Brave Writer

A Gracious Space: Fall Edition

Brave Writer LLC 7723 Tylers Place Blvd. #165
West Chester, OH 45069

Website: www.bravewriter.com

Brave Writer 2015

Author: Julie Bogart
Cover Photography: Tammy Wahl
Typesetting: Sara McAllister

First published in 2015

ISBN-10: 0990513327
ISBN-13: 978-0-9905133-2-2

Contents

Fall: A Gracious Space

Preface

A Gracious Space is a collection of thoughts and reflections on home education drawn from personal experience and the lives of thousands of Brave Writer families. The diversity found in the home education movement is its strength, despite the fact that at times, factions rise to evaluate, critique, and oppose one another. These daily readings are not aimed at a specific curriculum strategy, nor a singular homeschool philosophy. Rather, this volume is shaped by the belief that "home" ought to be a safe, kind, compassionate context for learning and family closeness.

Within that context, so much learning can and will happen—no matter what kind of personality you have or the learning styles your children exhibit. Homeschooling has a unique dynamic: we parents self educate as we home educate our kids; we enter that task blithely unaware of the challenges we will face. In relative isolation (without degrees, teacher in-service trainings, or a teacher's lounge) we educate our children with conviction and anxiety, enthusiasm and self-doubt.

All of us seek support—whether in the form of in-person cooperatives or online communities. This series of daily readings is drawn from the daily posts I've shared on the Brave Writer Facebook page. Apparently they struck a nerve: many of the entries generated hundreds of likes, shares, and comments. Parents wrote to ask if I could create a book so that they could read them when they needed that pick-me-up or that support from afar. This book is meant to be one of those supports.

This first volume has 50 entries for fall (one-third of a traditional school year). Two more editions have been released for winter and spring. Pair one per day with a cup of tea or coffee, and remind yourself of your values and your value. Each entry is accompanied by a comment from a parent like you and a daily sustaining thought.

Be kind not only to your children, but to yourself. You're a work in progress too—there is no "right" way to homeschool. There is only your journey as you discover, learn, implement, and adapt. The topics cover a range of principles and practices that apply to any homeschooling family. Embrace those that enliven and support you; skip the rest.

You might also find that these readings are useful at homeschool support group meetings. Read an entry as your meeting begins to give parents a perspective to consider for discussion or consolation.

Above all, enjoy the readings and your journey. The days pass slowly at first, and gather in speed as your children get older. The memories you are making now

Brave Writer

will be the inside jokes and happy stories you tell when your kids return to the empty nest on holidays.

Take a moment to reflect on the day before it gets underway. Receive the help and support that will give you the stamina to sustain the journey.

If you need more support on the journey, feel free to check out the homeschool coaching and mentoring program I offer at: http://coachjuliebogart.com. The Homeschool Alliance is designed to give you additional support and help you explore your vision to tailor-make your homeschool.

Enjoy this volume!

Keep going.

Day 1

A Unique Education

The hardest part of home education is that you, the primary responsible party, don't know how to measure your efforts. It's likely you grew up with a traditional school education. You remember that progress was evaluated through papers turned in, completed textbooks, solved homework problems, and test scores.

This new way of education feels too messy, amorphous, or filled with loose ends. The homeschooling parent can't appreciate that a long rich conversation with an eight-year-old about the blue jay at the feeder is better than three sentences written in a workbook about it. It's hard to think that the trip to the grocery store through the Asian food section (where everyone wonders about tubers and cabbage and why fish have eyes still in place) is more likely to create a connection to Asia than coloring in a map of countries. It's hard to believe that conversations over dinner about politics, values, history, and the latest movie really do teach, really do help kids form values, really do last longer in their imaginations than any set of quizzes or lectures.

Yes, you want your kids to master their math facts and to learn to spell. They will. The systems you're

 Brave Writer

using mostly work for most kids most of the time. What makes their education unique isn't how well you systematize all the subjects into a schedule. It's how well you share your enthusiasm for life, learning, art, literature, the power of math equations to create quilts or build forts or sell cookies, the excitement of an election year to convey the importance of politics, volunteering in your free time so that your kids learn about sharing themselves with others, and finally, your enthusiasm for them — these human beings entrusted to you that you admire, respect, and for whom you hold an enormous imagination about how well they will contribute to the world as adults.

Quote of the day

How apropos! Just this morning I was wondering how on earth I was going to make homeschooling work again this year! And, Julie, you did it again, reminded me how rich this life is and how worth the time and energy is to homeschooling my youngest daughter for yet another year! Thank you!

Monica McMaster

Sustaining thought

What makes your children's education unique isn't how well you systematize all the subjects. It's how well you share your enthusiasm for life, learning, art, literature, the power of math equations to create quilts or build forts or sell cookies, the excitement of politics, volunteering in your free time so that your kids learn how to share themselves with others, and most important, your enthusiasm for each of them.

Brave Writer

Day 2

It All Adds Up

It's so easy to feel behind, or like you aren't doing enough. In fact, when our kids are good at their schoolwork and get finished quickly (math page or copywork, grammar or reading), we might be tempted to undervalue the effort. We think: "It wasn't hard enough," or "She's rushing through it," or "This program is incomplete and too easy."

Then we find ourselves in the quick sand of reevaluation and angst— not satisfied with the evidence of progress, accomplishment, success, and achievement.

Honestly, we doubt success when we should doubt struggle. We overvalue struggle as evidence of learning, when if we really think about it, joy and pleasure are much better signs of learning and growth.

Isn't it strange? It's like we're never happy! My best friend in the homeschooling trenches used to say to me: "When my kids are outside playing, I wonder why they aren't at home reading a book. When they are inside reading a book, I wonder why they are wasting the sunshine and not playing outside. I'm never happy."

How true!

Our relentless need to push our kids (and ourselves), our insecurity about what progress looks like, and our memories of school (which are distorted by time and self-doubt), lead us to miss the evidence in front of our eyes—ease in learning, happiness in subject areas, brevity in finishing a task—these are evidences of successful education. Of course our kids will misspell or miscalculate. Of course they will sometimes use their worst handwriting or get distracted by a toddler who wants to play rather than finishing the chapter.

But that's okay too! All of it adds up to learning.

Today, instead of looking for what's missing, turn away from your fantasy homeschool vision. Notice reality. Make a list of all the things that go right today, such as:

- She brushed her teeth without my prompting her.

- He comforted his little brother when he started to cry.

- She finished her math page in ten minutes!

- He remembered which way the letter 'b' goes twice.

- She enjoyed listening to the read aloud.

- He wrote a list of materials to buy for his BB gun on his own!

- She practiced her dance routine.

- He went to his piano lesson and remembered to bring all the sheet music.

- She ate a good lunch.

Brave Writer

- He laughed a lot while watching TV.

- I got to spend five minutes talking to him about his favorite game.

- I helped her find her hair net and she was grateful.

See?

So much goes right every single day. All of it is education. Pace yourselves. Enjoy the periods where the "school part" feels a little too easy and the lessons, a little short, and the home, relatively functional and happy.

That's what you live for—don't forget to notice when it happens!

Quote of the day

It's crazy isn't it? I was talking with a friend about how I envied how "outdoors-y" and into exploring nature her kids are. She shared that she envies that we are so into kid lit and read so much together. I have to remind myself that it all "counts" even the stuff that comes naturally and easily (like kid lit for us—I'd read this stuff even if I did not have kids). Too easy to discount it. Building a foundation based on their strengths (what comes easily) actually makes it easier to work on the weaker areas.

Stephanie Hoffman Elms

Sustaining thought

Pay attention to the things that are working, to the peace you feel, to the smiles on your kids' faces, to the well being of your family. Value what you are doing well. Celebrate it! Trust that ease in your day is a sign that you are on the right path.

Brave Writer

Day 3

Educational Renaissance

Home educators share a little known secret. Most people assume we home educate because we distrust the school system or want to shield our children from growing up too quickly. Others think we homeschool because we are super religious types, or because we are super not-religious hippies!

Many of us start homeschooling for these reasons, and others, but here's the secret that most people *don't* know.

Homeschooling parents may start for any of those reasons—but home educators continue because we are getting a life-altering education at the same time!

When our kids ask to go to "real" school, we inwardly cringe. It's not the yellow bus we fear or the institutional classroom. Rather, we don't want our children to quit homeschooling because then we wouldn't get to read historical fiction for children or study art history the Charlotte Mason way or go on weekly nature hikes where we doodle in our journals. We wouldn't create lap books or celebrate the fall of Rome with artichokes and laurel wreaths. We wouldn't make cookies shaped like stars to go with the hot chocolate we sip while watching the Perseids meteor shower.

The truth is: once you get your homeschool chugging along, it's a runaway train, downhill! The enthusiasm to discover, learn, make connections, and explore takes over for everyone, but especially the home educating parent.

That's as it should be! The best homeschools are the ones where Mom or Dad can't put the book down.

You don't have to learn the same stuff as your kids either—you can tackle all the Jane Austen novels on audio book while making dinner (I did).

Embrace it. Own it. Follow personal rabbit trails. Learn. Grow. Live your excitement for the Civil War or Shakespeare or astronomy or algebra right in front of your kids, right alongside them.

The engine of your homeschool is fueled by your energy. It's the most delicious side effect of this enormous commitment. No one gets it on the outside looking in, but you know it on the inside. So relish your educational renaissance! You're earning it, one day at a time.

Cheers to you!!

Quote of the day

Caught me!!!

Dawn Ostgaard

 Brave Writer

Sustaining thought

Being a home educator means you not only get to educate your children, but you also have new freedom to further-educate yourself. Enjoy what you discover with your children. Your enthusiasm for learning drives your homeschool. But just as importantly, relish your newly catalyzed interests.

Day 4

No Magic Manual

Every day I get emails, phone calls, and online chats that ask me if Brave Writer has material that is "self-teaching." The parent asks me if they *have* to be involved, if there isn't some package of assignments the child can read and do alone, where the parent's only job is to give a grade or make final corrections.

They're looking for what I call the "Magic Manual"—the one that produces fabulous writers without effort from the parent.

No doubt moms and dads get exhausted from their deep involvement in homeschooling. However, writing is not the place to leave kids to their own self-teaching.

Let me rephrase that: You can't expect a child to learn to write without your partnership. Period.

The kids who are left alone to write without you—the dialog partner, the ally, the coach, and the editor—are unlikely to become quality writers. It's not the manual. It's not that they are lazy. It's that all writers (published, professional, best selling authors) need editors as partners. A second set of eyes is nice (for revision or editing), but a second brain for topic selection, idea generation, the

 Brave Writer

suggestions of resources, the practice of including specific literary elements, the pace of production, the varieties of genres available that would service the topic, are necessary, too, and must come from a parent.

If you, the parent, do not want to be a part of this process (and honestly, it continues into high school—it doesn't end at age twelve), then you need to hire someone to take that role in your child's life. Do not leave them alone. Do not berate them for a lack of motivation or progress. Do not expect a book or manual to teach. (The ones designed to teach without your help produce format writers, at best.)

You would never say no to talking with your child. Likewise, you need to dialog about the writing (talking on paper) with as much care and intentionality as you do with verbal conversation.

Brave Writer expects parental involvement because it is critical to growth in writing.

Quote of the day

> *Being an editor has always been natural for me, and being one 'professionally' for my kids has been so fun, freeing, and rewarding! I wouldn't trade this partnership for a self-teaching manual for anything. What a relief for me to have The Writer's Jungle as my manifesto so that what I've been doing all along is legit.*
>
> *Angela Palomo*

Sustaining thought

Your eyes, your brain, and your mentoring are crucial to your children's growth as writers. Your partnership offers assurance, encouragement, and practical help. Don't miss this shared experience of intimacy and creativity.

Brave Writer

Day 5

Be Good to You This Weekend

Congratulations. Another week in the books and another week of commitment to your wonderful family, completed. What will you do for yourself this weekend? Take a little time to be with you, on your terms.

Ways to look after yourself when you can't leave the children:

1. A bar of chocolate that you eat (no one else gets a bite). Pair it with tea or wine or Diet Coke (luxury, comfort beverage of your choice). Sneak it if you must (away from "May I have a bite, Mommy?").

2. A bath. Take the baby in with you, if you need to. Get in the warm water, add tear-free bubbles.

3. Read a poem alone. I like to do this at bedtime. It is nice by candlelight—after everyone is asleep. Light the candle, read the poem, be quiet. Notice the silence in the house before you crash into your pillow.

When you can leave for an hour, here are some pick-me-ups:

1. Take a walk alone, without dog, child, or baby in the backpack. Bundle up if it's cold and get into

nature (beach, woods, near a lake, on a bike trail). Breathe (take five deep slow breaths that fill the lungs). Take photos with your phone; notice the sky (the way it is huge and open) and the ground (the way it supports and holds you up). Remember your place in the universe. Be thankful.

2. Get to a library and hide in one of those private rooms (you may need to reserve its use). Bring a journal, a box of Kleenex, and reading material (iPad or book, magazine or devotional literature). Spend an hour alone with no agenda. Allow whatever is there to come up. Notice it, be with it, write it down, breathe it out. Pray, if you do. Say affirmations if that's what you do. This is your adult time-out.

3. Exercise: run, go to a spinning or Zumba class, ride a bike, sign up for a one-time yoga lesson.

When you can take a day (oh the gloriousness!):

1. Take yourself to an art museum sans children. Do it! It is the most incredibly satisfying experience. Roam the halls, pause, be moved, be quiet, let tears or smiles come and go freely. Go at your own pace. Like and dislike freely.

2. Sign up for a nature walk or go skiing for a day or join a hiking group. Be with people who don't homeschool but who do live out in the world! Explore, rub shoulders, and use your body.

3. See a double feature at the movies. Or go to a movie, followed by lunch or dinner alone, followed

 Brave Writer

by my favorite: coffee at Barnes and Noble, while I page through books.

Good luck! Be kind to you. You worked hard this week. You deserve some space to rest and know it.

Quote of the day

The delights of self-discovery are always available.

Gail Sheehy

Sustaining thought

Imagine an hour, a half-day, or a whole day all to yourself. What will you do? What will you observe? What will you feel? An adventure awaits you. Plan it now.

Day 6

No Shame on You

In the land of human beings, beware those who shame you for your failings, who urge greater fidelity to a system to cure what ails you rather than greater trust in yourself.

Beware those who put institutions ahead of persons, and whose idealism tempts you to pretend away your problems and distresses in favor of a sparkling seductive image.

There's no inoculation against life. Be as genuine as you can, try with the resources you have, open your mind to new solutions, and trust that you know what's best for you and your family more than anyone else does.

Take your time, be wary of unsolicited advice, and hold fast to your commitment to peace and well-being over ideology.

Sending love across the miles, in case you feel alone in your choices and dilemmas.

Quote of the day

> *Sometimes life is too hard to be alone, and sometimes life is too good to be alone.*
>
> *Elizabeth Gilbert*

Brave Writer

Sustaining thought

There is nothing shameful about loving your children, teaching them your values, holding them close. You know what's best, what brings your family peace and well being—regardless of what others say.

Day 7

Step Back and Observe

Did you realize that for no reason you can determine at the time, you will sometimes doubt your decision to homeschool?

It will come as a blindside, when you weren't even thinking about it. A random thought will sneak into your consciousness (her handwriting is wretched; he can't tie his shoes; she told me she hates reading; he is kind of awkward with kids his age; she doesn't have any friends other than our family; she's never interested in history; he hates practicing piano).

These little concerns grow as your mind gathers evidence to support the thought. Suddenly handwriting is the key factor in success or failure as a home educator.

You're no longer able to enjoy your child's quirks or successes because you can only see "This child is socially awkward!"

When your mind takes a 'scan for error' across the world of your homeschool, try to detach from the conclusions it suggests to you. Step back and observe the thought: *Oh there it is—that doubtful idea that threatens to undermine my confidence and energy for homeschooling.*

© Julie (Bogart) Sweeney | bravewriter.com Brave Writer

Be with it. Make it comfy: *So Johnny still can't tie his shoes. How about that? I wonder when he will? I wonder if he wants to? I wonder what would happen if I did nothing?*

Let that thought run alongside all the good happening in your family today.

Isn't it great that Johnny identified a new bird today? Look how sweetly he helped his sister get into her high chair. I loved the hug he gave me after lunch.

Breathe.

Then get a good night's sleep. Remember that all of us are suddenly knocked sideways by random thoughts on occasion—thoughts that make us spiral into doubt. Remind yourself that if your child were in school...

...you would still have random thoughts that tell you you are failing at parenting.

This is part of life (not homeschool specifically); this mental scan of flaws at home is a part of conscientious parenting. When you are troubled, keep the perspective that you can work on what worries you rather than using that anxiety to beat yourself up or reconsider your commitment to home educate. Guide your mind back to practicalities: ask questions about what's important, about the strengths of this lack, and whether there's a way to foster growth.

Remember: everything is less dire the next day, after a good night's sleep, breakfast, and a hot drink. Give the doubt room to move and breathe, but don't give it power to make your decisions. That's how you stay the course.

Good luck.

Quote of the day

I needed to hear this today. Right now. I have been having huge doubts this afternoon and was preparing to call our local middle school in the morning. I'm going to take a deep breath and get a good night's sleep. Thank you.

Rebecca Jackson Aydelette

Sustaining thought

Take a look at your doubt. Examine it and mull it over—but don't give in to it. Everything will look brighter after a deep breath, a cup of tea, and a good night's sleep. You're doing fine. Keep going.

Day 8

A Worthy Investment

We're all busy. We want short cuts, easy explanations, to do lists, and obvious, fast results.

Homeschooling doesn't work that way.

It's an investment—it takes time. Lots of time. Time you don't have.

When you decide to homeschool, you're choosing a degree program for yourself. You're choosing to become an autodidact (self-taught student) of learning—how it happens, under what conditions, using what tools, for which sorts of kids, in what subject areas.

To get a quality understanding of the nature of learning requires reading. A lot of reading.

It is on task to read email lists, homeschool bulletin boards, blogs, websites, curriculum books, the teacher's notes for any program you select, books about learning, homeschooling books about the philosophy of education, Charlotte Mason's education series, educators who have left the system to create new models of learning (Maria Montessori, John Holt), and more.

You have to do it. Most of us want to. Some of us worry that it will take too much time.

You can't think that way.

If you get impatient—"I don't want to understand the reasoning behind this program, I just want to know what to do"—you will, eventually, be frustrated by that program.

There is no "do this" and "it gets done" program. Each one requires knowing how to use it and what to do when there are blocks to progress.

Trained teachers spend years earning degrees to understand how to bring about the "aha" that signals learning in a classroom.

School has its own properties that require specific skill sets to create learning.

Home has other properties! These need to be studied, tried, lived, revised, tested, and measured against new information as you receive it. It is worth it (absolutely) to read the intent behind the philosophy before applying the practices.

If you are so busy that you don't have time to invest in training yourself to be a home educator, you must consider whether this is what you want to do with your life. Your kids deserve a parent at home who is well equipped to make learning an adventure that leads to joy and competence. They should not be subjected to

 Brave Writer

drudgery. Schools at least provide activities, field trips, friends, and variety.

We all need help. There's no shame in signing up for a co-op or tutoring, taking online classes or swapping with a friend. She teaches your kids math and you teach her kids writing.

You make decisions to involve others based on your philosophy of education, not because you don't want to do the work yourself. Even if you use a co-op, your involvement at home is critical. Parents of kids in school help their kids with homework every day. There are no shortcuts.

When you triangle-in help, involve passionate, competent people in the education of your children. I would rather have my kids learn how to shoot photos from my friend's husband who is a professional photographer than to teach them myself. I would rather swap math and language arts with my other friend since she's a whiz at calculus and conveys passion about math while I provide a similar experience with writing.

But in no case is it advisable to simply hand a child a book and ask that child to work through it—without you exerting some kind of effort to set up the lesson or to structure a context that makes that work meaningful.

I hear all too often that certain curricula (sometimes mine!) are too dense with philosophy or explanation about why and how the processes of learning work. The parents are busy. They want to get to the practices.

But does that work, really? What do you do when you barge ahead and the child winds up reluctant, resistant, or in tears? What do you do when the boredom of the daily practice turns into "cheating" (looking up answers in the back) to get done? What happens when you get to a process in the text that you don't "get" that had perhaps been explained in the opening?

There's absolutely no shortcut to homeschooling. It's an incredible undertaking of love and commitment—whether you unschool or use textbooks. In both cases, a sturdy, ongoing, investigation of how to problem solve and foster a love of learning will be your primary work for 15+ years.

It's great work! I loved it. Most parents who stick with homeschooling do.

But remember: when you are tempted to take a short cut, you may be circumventing the most important part of teaching—understanding why and how to create the right conditions for learning to catch fire.

Invest. The dividends are rich.

Quote of the day

What a great post! I am in my 13th year of homeschooling our five children. It is the best degree program I ever could have invested my life in. But just as checked in as I can be, I can also check out. That is when I have to re-evaluate and commit and check back in! I appreciate this wisdom.

Jonelle Rust Hughes

Sustaining thought

No shortcuts—rather an investment in your children and in yourself—to learn and grow and learn and grow some more.

Day 9

Competing Promises

It's not unusual to feel muddled when you think about what the best course of home education is for your children. There are competing promises among the many choices.

- freedom
- depth
- flexibility
- "children learn best when children decide what, when, and how they will learn, and for what purpose"
- advanced academic preparation
- mentoring
- "inspire, not require"
- connections between subjects
- personalized education
- "a well trained mind"
- "a science of relations"
- character building
- religion-free, multicultural, world citizen

 Brave Writer

- "literature-rich, Christ centered"

- "open-and-go"

- structured and thorough

- comprehensive

- parent-led

- child-led

I'm sure you can add quotes and slogans of your own.

With the advent of the Internet, there are even more homeschooling groups, websites, blogs, forums, email lists, and Facebook groups than ever. Each promises a happy, well-educated, well-adjusted child at the end of the journey.

When you explore, however, the advocates of any system typically believe in theirs so thoroughly, they disregard the value of any other system.

When you make a choice to adopt a specific program or plan (even if the "plan" is to let go of the "plan"!), the initial experience is often like trying to join a marathon in progress, only you've never done the training. You get tired, you say the wrong thing, you do the wrong thing—while the trained runners whiz by you.

Missteps and misunderstandings of the principles lead to strong exhortations on the part of the advocates: everything from advice-giving, to figurative hand-slaps, to humiliations.

Even when you earnestly seek to apply the principles in their entirety, if you run aground (have struggles, find that the method isn't working for one of your children, or discover that you aren't having the success you envisioned), sometimes you're blamed for not applying the principles correctly, or enough, or with the right tone of voice, or according to the right schedule (or lack of it!).

Learning how to live according to a vision someone else cast is demanding. No two people understand the vision the same way. Add your family to the mix (where you've done all the research, and they've typically done none), and you have a recipe for confusion—particularly during the transition away from one paradigm to another.

Parenting and education are broad categories. There is no one (single) way to bring children into adulthood as learned people. We know this because the world over uses a variety of parenting and educational strategies, and the world embodies brilliant minds and close connected families in cultures completely different from ours.

Our goal can't be to find the right set of tools, or the right ideology, or the right system. It can't be to advocate so righteously for one method that we overlook the benefit or valuable insights of another.

Any philosophy that adopts the viewpoint that if you experience failure or struggle, you aren't doing it right, is in danger of putting ideas ahead of people. No one lives any belief system so purely that they never run up against the limits of that perspective.

 Brave Writer

In fact, I'd go so far as to say that all perspectives have limits—and all people have limited abilities to carry out their best intentions.

Examining your principles is a good place to start (principles are easier to live by than rules). But purists can turn principles into rules, so be careful.

Your best bet is to be gentle with yourself and to surround your homeschool life with people who are advocates for you more than your philosophy of education or parenting. You should have room to air your confusion, your mistakes, your failures, and your successes. You shouldn't have to pretend to live up to the ideals of the group in order to participate. You shouldn't be subjected to unkind scrutiny for the sake of being a lesson for others.

It is possible to get value from a perspective, even if you don't adopt all of it.

It's possible to use a style of education for a few years, and then try something else for a few years just to change up the energy in your home.

It's great to read the powerful arguments for a variety of educational theories so that you avoid getting into a rut of thought where you make one view "all bad" and have to defend your view as "all good."

These are rarely useful ways to evaluate.

Finally, some seasons demand different styles of home education for everyone's peace of mind. Families dealing with chronic or terminal illness in a parent will necessarily approach home education differently than those with parents fully functioning.

What matters—what will matter most to you in the end—is the feeling that the people you love consider home and education to be pleasant, peaceful, and life-giving. No family or home feels like that all the time in any philosophy. Many philosophies help you get there. Most often, the philosophy is only as good as the emotional health of the parents anyway.

Your goal is to string together (like pearls on a necklace) moments where you can say, "Today was a good day together and we learned something too."

When these accumulate, life starts to hum. Don't worry so much about how you got there. Enjoy it while it lasts. Note it. Be proud of it. Don't doubt it.

Weirdly, that's enough—whether you co-sleep or bottlefeed or homeschool or put your kids on a yellow bus.

Love in the home, created by conscientious parents, who take education seriously (in any of its myriad forms), is what we all want.

Go forth into your homeschool today and enjoy whatever philosophy it is that fascinates you.

    Brave Writer

Quote of the day

Thank you for mentioning that even putting kids on a yellow bus can be enough. We are sending the kids to school next year after much wrestling with the idea, and I truly believe that for our family, for this particular time, this is the right decision. And we will still have lovely days when we love each other and learn something!

Emily Moothart

Sustaining thought

You're doing it right if you are a conscientious, loving parent, who takes education seriously (in any of its myriad forms).

Day 10

Content, Not Conventions!

Today's word advice: Don't be a grammar Nazi. It's so much more important to preserve/honor relationships, to receive the intended communication than to enforce proper usage in texting, FaceBook, freewrites, message boards, or any quick writing that does not rise to the level of permanence. Yes, every day people write "your" and mean "you're" or they write "here" when they mean "hear" or "loose" when they mean "lose." I "would of come" is hard to read. I admit. But if I say it out loud, I know what it means.

The purpose of all writing and speaking is to convey information, ideas, feelings, and thoughts. When someone risks self-expression and fails to get the grammar right, you can be the one who focuses on the content rather than the grammar conventions. If the issue recurs and it's someone you love, you can point it out in a gentle way days later: "By the way, did you know that it's 'would have' not 'would of'? Funny how the way we speak has made it hard to hear the original grammatical structure."

There's nothing inherently superior about being "right" about grammar. It just means you have that area of information mastered and someone else doesn't. So be

© Julie (Bogart) Sweeney | bravewriter.com Brave Writer

kind. Please. No one likes to be corrected for the errant apostrophe in "it's" or the mistaken "there." But all of us like to be heard.

Quote of the day

I have a bad habit of starting with the grammar errors rather than starting with encouraging comments on their content, which is often wonderful.

Heather Garson Gunraj

Sustaining thought

Content trumps grammar conventions in casual writing.

Day 11

Creating 'Aha' Moments

The best way to learn is when an "aha" moment is created. These usually come spontaneously when a connection is made and the little mental light bulb flashes You can facilitate that moment, though. It's not purely random.

Here are some ways to "flick the light on."

Cross-pollinate

As you make lunch today, ask your kids to help. When you're ready to pull ingredients from the pantry, ask them to assemble a lunch that tells you the story of _____.

The story could be the novel you are reading, the history you are studying, the scientific discovery you are learning about.

For instance, suppose you're reading about the solar system. Your kids might use star cookie cutters to create star-shaped cheese or sandwiches, and moon slices of apple. Name the stars. Arrange them in a constellation on your plate. Compare.

Find round fruits and vegetables to represent planets (could a pomegranate seed represent "Pluto" and a

© Julie (Bogart) Sweeney | bravewriter.com   Brave Writer

tomato "Mars" and a big honeydew melon "Jupiter"?). What foods do astronauts eat? Look it up online and see if you can make a facsimile. Talk about space and travel and the solar system all while making lunch! Maybe put it off until nighttime and do it for dinner.! You could use a telescope or just observe the stars through a window.

If you're reading about pioneers and Native Americans, you can make two lunches to choose from. Pick foods for each, talk about how you eat (with or without utensils, at a low or high table, off a plate or a rock or plank of wood).

Approximate the eating habits and the foods and the setting as you go about making lunch. Doesn't have to be perfect, just include everyone's input and do it together. Use Google to help you!

Use Your Bodies

Can your bodies be used to mirror punctuation as you read? What body movements can you use to signal exclamation points (a big jump, a hand clap, a high five)? Read a series of exclaiming sentences and every time you get to the end, do the body movement: High fives all around!

For commas, can you dip your head, drop open your jaw, take a big breath? How do you approximate "pause"?

Recite facts on the stairs. Whoever is answering gets to go down a stair for a right answer and up a stair when they miss. Keep going until you all get to the bottom.

Collaborate—if someone helps another to remember, they *both* get to go down a stair.

Throw a Frisbee or kick a soccer ball or toss pillows while reviewing times tables.

Create a Google Scavenger Hunt

Make a list of questions and send your kids to the computer to answer them. Can be competitive (whoever gets done first, wins a small prize). Can be collaborative (when all questions are answered by any and all together, everyone gets ice cream).

Answers can be handwritten or copied and pasted to a Word doc or written on a big white board (up and down from computer to white board, each person with their own color marker, creating a long list of answers/ facts). Set a timer and get them all answered before the timer dings!

You are not in *school*. You do not have to sit at *desks*. Lunch doesn't have to be a break from learning.

Get the light bulbs turned on! Takes energy. Create it. Use it.

Quote of the day

Hop off the straight and narrow when you can and take the winding paths.

Stacey Charter

© Julie (Bogart) Sweeney | bravewriter.com   Brave Writer

Sustaining thought

Mix things up a bit. Turn lunch into a culinary history lesson. Combine exercise with a grammar and punctuation review. You and your kids can make school whatever you want it to be. What freedom!

Day 12

Cut. Clip. Hug. Kiss.

Something to think about. All those hours you spend clipping, gluing, straightening, painting, organizing, planning, outlining, and listing…They're great because they're what you have to do.

But what will your kids remember? Connection.

Balance the work with relating (hugging, kissing, eye contact, and listening)…*every day.*

Quote of the day

A mother's love for her child is like nothing else in the world.

Agatha Christie

Sustaining thought

For every moment you spend planning and organizing, cutting, and clipping, take another moment to hug and kiss your kids—regardless of their ages.

 Brave Writer

Day 13

Do No Harm

You may not yet be acquainted with my writing guru, Peter Elbow. I frequently refer to him and his philosophy of writing. Here's one of his quotes I just love:

> *Most students benefit when they feel that writing is a transaction between human beings rather than an 'exercise in getting something right or wrong.'*
>
> *For this reason, I try to make my comments on student writing sound like they come from a human reader rather than from an impersonal machine or a magisterial, all-knowing God source.*
>
> *Thus:*
>
> *Instead of saying 'The organization is unclear here,' I like to say 'I got confused by your organization here.'*
>
> *Instead of 'unconvincing,' 'I'm unconvinced.'*
>
> *Instead of 'Diction,' 'Too slangy for me here.'*
>
> *Instead of 'Awk' (for awkward), 'I stumbled here.'*

Elbow's mantra in giving feedback is "at least do no harm."

One of the benefits of being a parent as writing coach is you can have conversations about the writing. You can say things to your child in the same manner you would talk about how to use the remote control or what to make for dinner.

"I loved this part. Got my heart pumping. I got a little lost here, but you got me back on track here."

"I wish I knew more about this person" and "I wonder what happens next!"

So much better than: "Focus on your tone" and "Your organization is hard to follow" and "You need more facts here."

The best coaching entices the writer to imagine new possibilities in the writing. That's different than asking your child to make improvements or changes so the paper is "right" or "correct."

Quote of the day

I love that Brave Writer helps me to translate what I now say into more relational jargon. Just changing a 'but' to an 'and' can make a world of difference! Thank you!

Angela Palomo

 Brave Writer

Sustaining thought

Today I choose to speak kind words to my kids, as a human being who loves them, not as an instructor correcting them.

Day 14

Don't Take it to Heart

Don't take it to heart when your efforts are under appreciated. Your investment is long term. The results will come in spurts or show themselves after years go by.

Don't take it to heart when your children are bored or tell you they hate homeschooling. It's a feeling, in the moment, shared with you because you are the safe place and the one in charge. Hold space for the feeling. But also hold space for homeschool. Sometimes the expression of frustration will subside, as they feel heard and supported. Don't make big changes after single outbursts. Stick with your plan, but offer compassion, support, and breaks.

Don't take it to heart when you try your best to apply principles that "work for everyone else" but aren't working for you. It's not you. Or rather, it is you—you matter. What works for you? Those principles and practices that ensure peace, progress, and passion. Check in with yourself and look for signs of life. Don't expect cookie cutter results applying someone else's practices and principles. Always find your own, or your version of the ones you admire.

 Brave Writer

Don't take it to heart when you have a bad day or a bad week or a bad month. We all go through dips and swings into the muddy places. Be good to you. Slow down, take a breath, regroup, and start again. If the dips and slides last longer than a month, pay attention. Discover the cause, but do so free of self-loathing or judgment. Solve the puzzle, not the crime. You aren't bad or wrong, just depleted and banged up.

Don't take it to heart when the email or forum post stings and zings, pops your bubble and misses the spirit of who you are. Online communication lacks emotional cues and gives too much permission to the expression of harsh feeling. Sip tea, read the comment, delete it or click out. Move on. You have too much to do and too many people to love to give that one invisible person power to disrupt your harmony.

Don't take it to heart when the progress you counted on doesn't emerge. You have time. There is always time—time for everything you've ever needed to do under the sun. You can't live as though there is no time. That posture squeezes the joy from living and hurries little people who can't be hurried and robs learning of its incubation and saturation stages. Be picky. Choose one thing at a time and trust it to teach everything.

Don't take it to heart when things go wrong, when you feel inadequate, when you are misunderstood, when you can't find your way. That's just today, just a moment. It will pass.

The kind of person who takes all these things to heart? A really good person, with a big heart. That's you.

Be good to you.

Quote of the day

I just went from feeling like a big, fat failure to feeling like a person with a really big heart. Thank you.

Michelle Uyterlinde Dwyer

Sustaining thought

When things go awry don't take it to heart. Instead give your heart a big hug!

Brave Writer

Day 15

Prophecies of Doom

We've all made them—those pronouncements that let our children know that the perilous choice they make today will land them in a low-paying ditch of a job, eking out a half life, regretting that they didn't master the proof for right angles on the third Thursday of September.

The slow descent to adult failure begins when the precious cherub who suckled at your breast defies your plan for his life.

You see him happily writing poems instead of completing math tests (yes, that would be my son Noah) and declare: "How will you get into college if you never advance in math?"

He plays around with sign language, studies Klingon, and never takes chemistry.

Dire predictions follow: "You must complete high school. You can't expect colleges to make exceptions for you. Without a college degree, you won't ever earn enough money to live."

Except that colleges do make exceptions, and they make them for your son, who they told to put Klingon on his transcript for his foreign language requirement, and apparently the linguistics department doesn't care whether or not he took chemistry in high school.

You proclaim to your daughter that she must study U.S. history because no college will accept her without it on her transcript. She never musters the interest. U.S. history study lags and flags and sputters. When it's time to apply for college, she does a six-week crash course and is accepted into the scholars program at the university of her choice.

You declare that no one can live on minimum wage—and then your adult child does, somehow (maybe not to the standard of living you'd want for him, but he makes it work because it's his life and this is what he wants for now).

We tell our kids they will get lost if they don't print directions; we tell them they will lose all their teeth if they don't brush them; we warn that if they don't sleep eight hours a night, they won't be able to think straight the next day.

We predict that no girl will ever kiss our son if he doesn't learn to shower. We declare that online friends aren't real friends and so our child is friendless.

We make sweeping statements out of fear and love, I know. We all do it.

Last night a mother I spoke with told me that her nine-year-old son had just begun to lie to her, for the first time in their precious intimate close self-aware

© Julie (Bogart) Sweeney | bravewriter.com   Brave Writer

relationship. It stunned her. She launched into the parental "never lie to me" prophecy of doom: "How can you lie to me? We will never have trust again if you don't tell me the truth. You are ruining our relationship."

But that's not what is happening. A nine-year-old boy is avoiding something, has figured out that if he tells half the truth, he may only have to do half the work. It's not likely he intends to destroy the parent-child bond—but we frame it that way. We get big and dramatic and huge and sometimes even loud and lecture-y and oh how we love to go for length in those moments.

Parents aren't stupid. They have made so many mistakes in their 35-50 years on the planet, they only want one thing: for their children to not make any. Parents can see further down the time line. Sometimes that's an enormous advantage! Kids do well to heed parental vision!

But not every time. Not about every thing.

Not all the choices your kids make today need to match the ones you would have them make.

In fact, I'll go further. Our biggest job isn't to prophesy doom or to spell out impending disaster or to nudge, nag, and coerce cooperation with our vision for their lives (or even what we are convinced is their vision for their lives).

Our job is to be pointers. It's better to say stuff like:

"Hmm. You don't want to take more math? I wonder if UC will accept you into their program if you were to apply without it. Let's call to find out. What if you don't call and don't take the math? How would you feel if they didn't accept you because you didn't take pre-calc? Would you take it then? Where?"

We need to help our kids think about the choices they are making, not tell them the outcome of the choices before they've made them. We can point our children in the right direction—suggesting they find out what they don't know and honestly, what we may not know either.

When Noah stuffed his transcript into the application envelope for college, he said the following: "I'm going to be so mad at myself if not taking chemistry keeps me out of college."

That's what you want to hear! Noah knew it was his choice, one he made with full information—that most kids need chemistry in high school to qualify for college.

And wouldn't you know? His wager won. He was accepted to the linguistics program without chemistry.

The main reason you don't want to prophesy doom is because you don't know how things will turn out. You really don't. But you do have valid concerns and some perspective and a slew of ideas about how to make a satisfying life. Your best bet is to engage in conversation, point out things to consider, and even to prophesy a little hope:

 Brave Writer

"I would hate to study chemistry too. In fact, I never did! We didn't have to take that class in high school when I was your age. I wonder if there's a way to get around it. I wonder, if it is required, if there's a way to do it so it's less annoying. But I know you. You're smart! You'll get to where you want to go eventually, and I want to help you get there. Shall we do a little research before we abandon the traditional path? Just to be sure?"

Resist the temptation to prophesy doom.

Establish the habit of research and considering all options. Give support, faith, and love.

Then see what happens.

Quote of the day

What a wonderful piece. It made me laugh and it made me think. Thank you. It hit me right in my heart and I listened. I prophesy doom. "If you don't do this today, then XYZ will happen in your future." Mmmm food for thought.

Cybele Harris Botran

Sustaining thought

Doom and gloom? Or discuss and discover? What works best in your family?

Day 16

Drafting and Sharing

Create a home environment where people do what they do, near each other. I call this "drafting" off of each other's interests. As one watches a movie or reads a book, someone else is online posting to a discussion forum. Someone else may be putting together quesadillas and still another, folding laundry.

If you inhabit a space together, you can pitch in, shout out a momentary insight, read a tidbit from your book aloud, call attention to a funny pun on a TV show, ask a question, or share a new fact. Learning happens when you draft off each other's absorptions, and enjoy shared spaces.

Quote of the day

We have a big house, but everyone hangs out in the same room, reading or playing with iPods or doing things that could be done in separate rooms. Even the almost-teen prefers to do her own thing surrounded by the rest of the family.

Ellen Gribosky Horner

© Julie (Bogart) Sweeney | bravewriter.com

Sustaining thought

Cozy spaces near those you love don't just show up. But you can create them. Find places in your home to do what you do while your kids do what they do—close to one another. Then let the conversation flow and notice the rich sharing that results.

Day 17

Growth in Writing

Today's reminder about writing: Growth occurs through a series of writing attempts. Growth is not solely dependent on completions, though going all the way from thought to final edited product ought to happen a couple times a year per child.

Your job is to create writing opportunities that match your child's developmental stage, and to support his or her attempts. Then, once in a while, bring a project all the way through the revision process and a final edit of mechanics.

You'll notice growth over time, not in every project. You'll notice a trajectory of development, comfortableness with the process, and pride in the projects you complete together.

Quote of the day

You fail only if you stop writing.

Ray Bradbury

 Brave Writer

Sustaining thought

Your homeschoolers will grow in writing over time just as they grow in weight and height—over time. Be patient. Be supportive. Watch for the surprises along the way.

Day 18

Happiness Is…

I read a blog the other day that reminded me: Happiness is not a completed puzzle with all the pieces glued into place, varnished, framed, and then hung on the wall—as though once you find that last piece and arrange it in the missing space, completing the puzzle "just so," you will have achieved happiness and that quest will be finished.

It makes a great 'picture' but can happiness really be contained in a still, framed, lifeless image?

It's so easy to think that if I pad my cell with the right set of philosophical bumpers, I will avoid sharp objects and intrusive voices that wreck my peace.

I thought about it more.

Happiness at home, as I've observed it, is the experience of being okay with my homeschool the way it is today—unfinished, messy, incomplete—spilling out the sides, running down the legs of the table, and busting through the neatly graphed lines of my schedule.

So that's the problem with "joy in the journey" thinking. We still try to get somewhere so that we'll finally feel justified in feeling happy.

© Julie (Bogart) Sweeney | bravewriter.com Brave Writer

What if "happiness" is utterly different than we've been led to believe by advertisers, gurus, and advice-givers?

Happiness in my homeschool looks like slathering a big thick layer of yummy love across my imperfect self and my silly, sometimes struggling, sometimes thriving bunch of little rascals that live their own version of happy in the middle of the mess.

It's forgiving myself for my lack and inadequacy and recognizing that I don't have all that it takes to homeschool. Some days I don't even have half of what it takes.

Happiness comes when I'm least expecting it—when a moment stirs me or catches me off guard, like a hug and kiss, or a brand new word read, or a note pinned to my pillow, or a pair of kids playing without arguing for ten whole minutes.

It comes when I give up, give in, and let today be what it is. It comes when I trust that tomorrow will by okay, too, and I can look back at yesterday and think, "That wasn't all bad. It looks even better in hindsight..."

Happiness is a state of being, not a goal achieved or a mindset created or a philosophy rigidly followed. It comes when you let go and float and let the waves of your life ride.

Think of labor—yielding, trusting, crests, and valleys. But oh so good, and leading to the oh so right, and messy too.

If you're in that space of self-recrimination, where you can't figure it out, can't identify what's going wrong, if you wish you were better at being a mom or teaching math or having big juicy conversations—stop. Go inside and let yourself fall apart a little bit.

Be good to you. Accept who you are—wrap that hurting self in a pair of big strong arms. You're okay. I know you want to grow and change and be better. We all do. One way to get there is to stop trying to fix it. Simply be where you are, as you are, living with the magical people entrusted to your care.

You don't have to solve it. You can keep going, you can embrace the uniqueness that is your life, trusting that over time, everyone will find their way when you stop pushing so hard to make it all fit into that framed puzzle.

Happiness may find you yet.

Quote of the day

I really love this, Julie. Fits so many aspects of our real, messy lives. Especially for women, with our tendency to judge ourselves so harshly. Especially (right now for me) in reference to our bodies. Love them now, as they are. In process, fluid. Thank you.

Debbie Nielsen

 Brave Writer

Sustaining thought

Make a mess loving and being.

© Julie (Bogart) Sweeney | bravewriter.com 61

Day 19

Help is Near; Ask for It

If mothers could learn to do for themselves what they do for their children when these are overdone, we should have happier households. Let the mother go out to play!

Charlotte Mason

Teach your children to meet your needs, just as gladly as you meet theirs. Ask for their help.

For instance, if your day feels bleak and dreary, you can ask your children to make you a centerpiece of wildflowers and then send them out to find the bark, moss, and periwinkle.

If you are beleaguered, you know that tea cures all. Ask a child to put on the kettle.

Ask your children to set a beautiful table for lunch, using the special placemats.

Ask an older child to set the timer, and then lead a five-minute "spruce up" of the living room to loud music.

You can ask your kids to toss a Frisbee with you in the fresh air.

You can all make sock balls that you toss into a clean waste can at the end of laundry folding to score points.

Ask your children to lay a washcloth across your forehead when you have a headache and to add a little lavender oil.

Ask them to use Pledge and the dusting cloth to wipe down all the dusty wooden surfaces. (Kids love this!)

Asking for help is different than assigning chores. Drop the "assignments" and "demands" and "lectures about responsibility," and literally *ask for help*.

You might frame it like this:

"Wow. I'm exhausted today and a little overwhelmed. You know what would help me?...."

Then say it. Children love to make you happy and helping you is the chief way they can.

When you are overdone, get help or go play—or do both. Charlotte Mason says so, and so do I.

Quote of the day

Love the idea of asking children to give back. What a great lesson for them as they move forward.

Loving With Purpose

Sustaining thought

Trade assigning chores for asking for help. Discover the pleasure of receiving from your children who are eager to show you their love.

Brave Writer

Day 20

Wishful Thinking

If you can't give your child what she wants, you can give it to her in a wish.

For instance, if she tells you she wants her own horse (yet you live in an apartment and don't have the funds or lifestyle to support a horse), you don't need to crush the vision with practicalities. Instead, give it to her in a wishful fantasy.

Wouldn't it be wonderful to own a horse?

What would you name it? Where would you ride it? What would it look like? Do you know what type of horse you'd want to own? Shall we look them up online and see?

Would you want to show the horse in competitions? Ride the horse over jumps? Learn dressage?

Or would you prefer to ride bareback alone over hills looking at the sunset?

Of course you don't simply shoot questions at her as if pulling the trigger to a BB gun. You want to give her the chance to live her fantasy with you for a little emotional vacation. Let her describe the horse's mane and color, where she would ride, how she would care for the horse, why a horse would be such a dear companion at this stage in her life.

If possible, assist the fantasy with practical possibilities even if they fall short of the ultimate fantasy:

- Maybe we can ride horses at the local stable this month.

- How about we check out some good old films about horses and watch those over the next week?

- Let's pick a horse to follow in the upcoming series of horse races and get to know its life story.

- I know there's a saddle shop in town. Maybe we can learn how they are made, feel the smooth leather with our hands, and ask about local horseback riding while we're there.

- I wonder if we can take a family vacation to a dude ranch one year.

- Our homeschool group may have a family with a horse we can visit. Let's ask.

The thing about kids is that they enjoy possibilities far more than we do. They aren't jaded, haven't had their dreams dashed, don't manage the checkbook, aren't limited in their energy. There's no need to "smack down a dream" before it has a chance to emerge. Give it some breathing room—allow it to manifest in conversation, illustrations, reading, narration, writing, and play. Then find the little

Brave Writer

pieces of the fantasy that you can support/provide, and find a way to incorporate these into your child's life.

Sometimes magic happens and the little bit of wind you blow into those sails leads to the fulfillment of the bigger dream, too. Kids have a way of conjuring wonderfulness from nothing, which is one of the reasons we love having them in our lives.

Wishful thinking is a gift, not a thing to be disparaged.

Quote of the day

> I've never thought to do this before but I love the idea. Thank you. I do remember that my own mother used to respond to some of our over-the-top wishes with, "How many would you like?" That usually produced a laugh from me.
>
> *Jordan Laird Foley*

Sustaining thought

While helping your child indulge in a bit of wishful thinking, how about giving in to some of your own? Possibilities drop into open spaces—when we give our dreams space to grow and manifest.

Day 21

How You Say it Matters

Remember when you went into labor (or if you adopted kids, remember the stories your mother and friends have told you about birth)? Usually there's quite a bit of emotion, physical pain, anxiety, and apprehension.

What if your husband or partner joined you during labor and said the following in a "take charge" (perhaps even coercive or condescending voice)?

"Sweetheart, I know this is scary and hard, but you have got to get a grip! Millions of women for thousands of years have given birth to babies. You're no different. Now you get in there and have that baby. I don't want to hear another word of complaint from you. I've got things to do and when I come back, I expect that baby to be here. Now get going."

How would you feel? Would you be planning a call to the lawyer? Considering ways to short sheet the bed?

What if, instead, you heard these words, delivered in a sympathetic voice?

"Sweetheart, I know this is scary and hard. I see you are in pain. Millions of women for thousands of years have

© Julie (Bogart) Sweeney | bravewriter.com   Brave Writer

given birth to babies. They have all felt like you do right now. The baby will come. All you have to do is trust the process. I'll be here, right by your side, holding your hand when it gets tough, distracting you when it helps. And I promise, at the end of this arduous process, there will be a baby so precious to us we'll both declare that it was all worth it. No matter what, I'm here to support you."

Which one do you want at your bedside? Husband A or Husband B?

Which type of parent do you think your children want when they embark on a writing project?

"Kids everywhere have to write and they all complain about it. That's no excuse. I have things to do. Now you get in there and write three sentences. They had better be written by the time I get back! I don't care that you hate writing. You just have to do it."

or

"Kids everywhere have struggled to put pen to paper while thinking of things to write. You are just like them. It's okay. I'll be here with you, holding your hand, helping you think about what to say, how to say it, and reminding you of what you want to write so that you can get your wonderful thoughts out onto the page. We'll do as much as we can today and take it up again tomorrow. I'm here to help. At the end, the writing product will be so worth it. You'll see."

Remember: don't minimize pain or misinterpret it as laziness. Usually, the dawdling and whinging (love that word) is more about a lack of support in the process. Remind your child that the pain they feel is legitimate and natural, and that there are ways through the jungle to the other side. Remind them that you are their companion for the journey, have tips and tricks to help, and that you don't mind at all.

That's a great place to start.

Quote of the day

Thank you for sharing!!!! Way new perspective and I have been trying to find a better way to give support and courage than the "Husband A" way.

Hannah Cole

Sustaining thought

What you say is important—but how you say it is essential!

© Julie (Bogart) Sweeney | bravewriter.com   Brave Writer

Day 22

In Defense of the Disillusioned

Sometimes your life doesn't work out how you planned it,

line by line,

promise by promise,

heart beat by heart beat.

Sometimes the vision that dances in your head
like sugar plums and happily ever afters and smart,
successful, contributing citizens called your children,
turns into a puzzle you can't solve or a missing piece
you can't find under the cushions or that thud thud in
your chest…

…a persistent "something's not right, something's not
right" that clicks with your heels and follows you into the
grocery store.

Sometimes the ideal shatters through no obvious fault
of your own (though you wish it were so you could fix it,
naturally, like you fix everything else)—someone else's
implacable will thwarts/harms/crushes yours or finds
happiness in someone else's.

Sometimes your body succumbs to germs or cells that won't stop growing and they take over your organs and ruin your chance to do all you had planned for forever and a day. Sometimes they live in the body of your dearest friend, deepest love, or most beloved child.

Sometimes, no matter how diligently you protect them and worry on their behalf, your children stumble into tragedy or crime unimagined and never planned.

Sometimes one of your precious kids is violated horribly while you were pinning new kitchen photos to Pinterest and having devotions.

The disillusioned suffer twice and three times.

Not only do they face the excruciating pain of tragedy, at night, and in the middle of the afternoon. They also face the natural tendency of those we love most to assign blame for the failure.

Pain, loss, divorce, disease, violation—to the not-yet-suffering, these are as contagious as mumps or the common cold. All who are not afflicted look for the cause so they can stay safe and not make the horrible mistakes you've made.

You didn't do it right.

You didn't pray enough, go to therapy, read the right books, get the right doctors, eat the right foods, follow the right advice, use these steps, take this tone, follow this

 Brave Writer

practice, behave in that way, honor this code, believe that set of precepts…

The list goes on endlessly and no protestations of how much you tried calms the advice-givers. They want to believe they have identified the one or ten key ingredients that you missed, that they can embrace, to avoid your fate.

They don't try to figure out your failings to be cruel. Know that. It's desperation. To avoid your tragedy.

But you can face this disillusionment—this failed bargain with God or life or nature—differently because these awful conditions are real for you. Not theory. Not avoidable. They're here now, waiting for you to deal with them, not with what you "might have done" or "could have done differently."

Disillusionment is the beginning of new chances—a chance to find a new way to live or love, for however long you have.

It's the beginning of asking real questions rather than seeking iron-clad answers.

It's your chance to take some risks, to explore some forbidden secret ideals you had overlooked before in your safety.

It's your chance to have an authentic, self-created journey rather than the second-hand one the books and leaders tell you to have.

It's a chance to pay attention to people as they actually are rather than as you wish them to be.

It's often your first real chance to ask yourself: Who am I? And then another better chance to become that person in a whole new way.

I love talking with disillusioned homeschoolers because they are closer to being good at educating their kids than the ones who think they have a "system that works." If homeschooling has failed you somehow, if your marriage is not working, if your children are reacting against you and you don't know how to bring them near, you are much closer to having a life built on a foundation of truth and reality than you've ever been.

Hold on. Face life on its terms: the pain, the disillusionment. Don't judge your life. Pay attention to it. Let it tell you what you need to know. And by all means, find others who've walked similar journeys. They will have wisdom to share.

You are not bad, wrong, or a failure.

You are not foolish, uncommitted, or selfish.

You are human. Everyone, by the time they get to 50 or 60, will have experienced the humbling realization of being time-bound and planet-dwelling among germs and people.

 Brave Writer

That you would attempt (for example) to be married (till death!), to have children (to home educate!), and to love your life (despite cancer!) is brave and optimistic.

Draw on those resources as you face your disillusionment squarely.

Then see what happens. You might be amazed.

Quote of the day

I feel like I have experienced this in so many ways, Julie. Thanks for articulating it so beautifully.

Ann Herndon Corcoran

Sustaining thought

Life delivers its blows no matter what we do—but it also brings inexplicable blessings no matter what we do. Embrace both.

Day 23

It's Not Too Late

It's not too late to teach writing or fractions or a love for reading.

It's not too late to have big conversations or to show interest in your children's noisy music or boring card games.

It's not too late to sketch the trees or recite poetry.

It's not too late to study chemistry or learn calculus or play a musical instrument.

It's not too late to be gentle, or to listen more attentively to your child.

It's not too late to get help for your struggling learner, no matter how old he or she is.

It's not too late for therapy or support groups or help for you. It's not too late to make the hardest decision you'll ever make.

It's not too late to go on the field trip or save money for the special camp or to go on the big vacation to the place you imagined you'd all go.

It's not too late to learn more about home education.

© Julie (Bogart) Sweeney | bravewriter.com   Brave Writer

It's not too late to change course, revise your plan, or to try something new.

It's not too late to have the homeschool you imagined, even if you try it just for a day, or a week, or a whole month to see how it goes.

You can start today, or tomorrow, or even next week. You can start in the fall or after Valentine's Day or once the baby is born.

If it doesn't go the way you'd hoped, it's not too late to go back to how things were.

If it's harder than you expected, it's not too late to take more time, or go more slowly, or get help.

If you love the new direction or find that you're making progress or see that your children are thriving, it's not too late to be proud of that choice!

You don't have to regret that you didn't figure it out sooner, or that you weren't made aware of this wonderful new resource, path, or philosophy. Congratulate yourself on finding it now, on having the courage to stake out a new footpath for you and your family.

It's never too late to do what you want to do…now.

Quote of the day

I find I have been saying this to myself for sometime. I have been changed by dealing with special needs children. I have grown as a person because of this. It's never too late for anything since as individuals we all have different timelines and awakenings. It's truly amazing to have an aha moment.

Roslyn Taylor

Sustaining thought

Drop the guilt, take a risk, address a need. It's never too late.

Brave Writer

Day 24

It's the Relationship, Sweetheart

When you're tempted to get worked up about algebra, breathe. Remind yourself:

My daughter and I can tackle algebra more easily if we like each other.

When your son spills the Cheerios right after you told him to wait for you, hold back. Let the lava flow of irritation run through you, but don't spill it onto his little head. Remember:

He won't always spill Cheerios, but he will be grateful that I'm not the type to lose my cool.

When you can't squeeze another chapter into the end of the year, and you're disappointed in yourself for not being more disciplined, let go. Notice:

My children like me. I like them. I can let that be enough, because it is.

When heartbreak threatens to steal your memories, when you don't know how to get to the next space because it's unfamiliar and riddled with loss, hold on. Tell yourself:

It will be okay because I love and am loved. I'll get to the other side by loving, not by fearing.

When one of your children doesn't like you right now, trust. This too shall pass:

My love and like are big enough for the both of us. I can let my natural devotion and affection lead me, not my resentment, nor my anxiety, nor my anger.

When you imagine your children in the future, what do you see? Inside jokes, vacations at the beach, memories of outings taken and books read, big hugging reunions, foods to share, and games to play? Pay attention:

These start now. I can do them now. I will value them now.

In the end, the book learning will come (sometimes quickly and ahead of schedule, sometimes in college, sometimes not until one of your children decides to home educate his or her offspring). What can never be scheduled or studied, crammed or tested is love.

Homeschooling is a performance of love between family members over a sustained, daily, intimate period of years, led by a parent who puts relationship ahead of books.

Check in with yourself today. Be present to your children. Love one another.

Brave Writer

Quote of the day

Beautiful—sent with a renewed and thankful heart.

Jeanette Weiler

Sustaining thought

It's all about love—and love is enough to sustain everything else.

Day 25

Know Your Kids as They Are

Recently, I read a plea from a desperate mother of a nine-year-old girl who hates school. The mother felt helpless, hurt, and angry. She appealed to her email loop for support and advice. The first email reply went through the "nurturing model":

- *rock her in a rocking chair,*
- *don't worry about school,*
- *she's young still,*
- *enjoy precious moments,*
- *help her to feel comfortable and happy in your home with less school pressure*

The very next reply was a 180-degree turn. This mother offered a list of quotes out of *Train up a Child*. The first one said roughly, "Don't make rules you won't enforce." And of course, if you make a rule, require obedience. Suggestions of penalties followed:

- *time outs,*
- *wooden spoon spankings,*
- *withdrawal of TV or computer privileges.*

© Julie (Bogart) Sweeney | bravewriter.com   Brave Writer

These two positions were so opposite to one another, I found myself laughing out loud. What kind of parents are we? It seems to me that the real issues are often missed in these discussions. We parents are quick to evaluate the behavior of our kids and then to look to each other for "tricks" or "tips" on how to "deal with them." The desperate mother is asking the wrong questions to the wrong people.

The Inner Lives of Our Children

The inner lives of our children ought to be the object of our quest. When they throw routine tantrums and say outrageous hurtful things, why aren't we asking where that's coming from? So often we just want to squelch the behavior—extinguish it like a sputtering candle. Can we know our kids from the inside out? Will they talk to us? Some kids have no trouble telling us their needs or hardships. Others are completely tongue-tied-stuck, perhaps in the non-verbal mode of relating to themselves, aware of problems and feelings but unable to articulate them or even to identify them.

Instead of rules enforcement versus nurturing to the point of "catering to," how about investigation and support/compassion? How about encouragement and understanding? Are we willing to know our kids as they actually are rather than to simply apply labels for behavior, or symbols for their season of life, or rules for their "own good"? What if we become fascinated by the complexity of our kids, rather than worried by them?

Sweet Noah

I remember when Noah (my oldest) was 10 years old and he struggled with writing. His attitude showed that he was demoralized (even after all I've done for him to make it easier). My ego got flustered and irritated.

He was violating my system.

He was invalidating my work.

But my spirit knew differently. I suddenly saw that Noah must have had real reasons that made sense to him about why writing was challenging. It was a moment. I flipped my point of view away from wondering where I went wrong or why he couldn't validate my efforts to what was going on inside of him. So I asked him with gentleness and true interest:

"Noah, what's wrong? What is bothering you?"

Do you know that for the first time, tears of shame and earnest self-displeasure surfaced? He felt badly that he couldn't please me by "getting it" more quickly.

This reminded me of feelings I had as a girl when my father tried to help me with math homework and I just didn't get it. My dad got so frustrated with me, thinking he'd been clear (I'm sure he had been).

 Brave Writer

But I felt desperate inside. I couldn't validate him. I could only fail in his presence and make him miserable. What an awful feeling–to know your parent is trying to help and you can't translate that help into success! The only way forward is to shut down, if there is no entry point for discussion or honest communication of scary internal feelings. I feared I wasn't smart. I didn't want my dad to know that about me. So I clammed up.

Noah's weren't tears of frustration or anger or anxiety about writing specifically. I could tell. He said to me, *"You're a writer. You and Dad talk about it all the time. You teach it. No matter how much you tell me that you aren't worried about how well I write, I still know that you'd be happier if I wrote well. And I want to do it but know I can't."*

More tears.

Wow! So honest. So risky!

The only respectful reply at that point was silence. I saw. I didn't have an explanation, or more information to throw at him, or even good ideas, or defenses for how wrong his perceptions were. I saw. And in seeing, I knew that all I really had to offer was compassionate support. A hug. A kind, understanding smile of sympathy.

So I told Noah that I loved him, appreciated his openness in risking those words out loud, and I offered to do whatever it took to support him in finding his own way out of those oppressive feelings. It was a moment.

My Real Job at Home

I discovered that my true job as a mother was to care more than anyone else about the interior lives of my kids. I wanted to be there to watch, encourage, and do what it took to support them in triumphing over the hurdles they faced. Noah gave me a gift. He articulated his feelings in a way that I could understand. Lucky me! Here was an instance where Noah's self-awareness and verbal capacity helped him. Realizing that he could find his words when he felt safe and cared for, helped me know he'd write well one day.

Not all of our kids can express themselves as easily in words. We want to remember to listen beneath the words, or to help find the words for our other kids when they get that stuck. Or at minimum, we can offer a comforting response like, *"It must be so frustrating to not be able to express what's bothering you right now."*

Noah and I talked for 45 minutes the next day about his writing project on roller coasters that he'd begun, and the change was dramatic. He felt freer to ask for help, to try my ideas, and he knew I was relaxed and happy with him. We did the work together, and I watched him go to the computer to write with relief and success. I was humbled by that. It struck me that he found a way to relieve the pressure of those "illegal" feelings, and then with my kindness and companionship, writing followed.

 Brave Writer

That may not be the exact sequence in your family. However,

  relief,

    light,

      hope,

        intimacy,

          and optimism

may follow.

Those are good too.

Quote of the day

I believe I am my children's cheerleader, their coach, and adviser. I learned early on that getting down on my knees and looking into their eyes, heart to heart, was the most powerful and effective way to communicate. They responded the greatest at these times. They hugged me and thanked me, and over the years they have learned they can come to me about anything.

Natalie

Sustaining thought

Taking time to explore your kids' feelings when they feel stuck can be the way through to the words they long to express in speaking and in writing.

Brave Writer

Day 26

Less is More—Really!

The tricky part of homeschooling, and particularly writing, is that you can't see the growth as it happens. Looking back shows you the growth. But looking back happens when our children head off to college, or Europe, or get married. That feels a teensy bit late.

In other words, the very thing you need to reassure you that you are doing a good job with your kids is invisible to you as you do that "good job with your kids." You're required to put your faith in the process, rather than confidence in observable results. (Or, alternatively, you have to change how you measure what you see.)

It really is enough to read aloud to your kids, to have your children copy some of those words into a little notebook, to have them take a stab at writing some of those words without looking while you dictate them aloud. It's enough if this happens once a week or twenty times in a year, and some years even fewer times.

It's enough to catch a few of children's brilliant thoughts or quirky ideas in writing for them, once in a while, so they know that what's inside them deserves to be on paper too.

It's enough to linger at dinner, discussing some topic like the puns in Seinfeld or why *Pocahontas* the Disney movie, is both so good you want to keep watching it but so bad (if you compare it to history) that you feel guilty for loving it.

It's enough to lie next to your kids at bedtime once in a while to sing to them or listen to their stories or to tell them some ridiculous saga you made up that goes on and on and stops making sense after a few weeks but you both love just the same.

It really is enough if your kids read and read and read the same book series over and over again and it seems like they will never discover another author as wonderful as JK Rowling or Brian Jacques or Suzanne Collins or Ian Fleming or Jeff Kinney. One day you'll notice, oh hey! She's reading another book by someone else.

It's enough if you listen to what your kids say, if you have big juicy conversations about the stuff that interests them, if you laugh at funny sounding words and use absurdly big ones around them just to trick them and tickle their linguistic imaginations.

It will be enough if they read a little poetry, look up a few song lyrics, memorize a couple tongue twisters, learn to tell a few really funny jokes, and figure out the delicious humor of Will Shakespeare in one of his comedies (in a movie of course).

 Brave Writer

It's enough if they cast their thoughts onto a page, freely, attending only to the ideas or the sound of the words, and know they have a receptive audience in you.

It's enough if they play with other writing forms, if they learn how to mop up their own mechanics, if they attempt half a dozen essays in high school, figuring out what it means to have a point of view that they assert and then how to back it up because it matters to them.

We make it so difficult. We expect our kids to match some other agenda than the one that delivers them happily into an authentic writing life.

Less is more—less hand-wringing, fewer assignments, less control, less nagging, fewer criteria.

More is more—more conversations, more reading, more delight, more time, more space, more passion for language, more opportunities to play with words.

I'm here to help when you lose your nerve or your way.

Quote of the day

Love this. It makes language development, or literacy as I like to call it, so real to life and less like a school subject.

Linda Dempster

Sustaining thought

Less planning and more spontaneity results in happy moms and happy kids!

 Brave Writer

Day 27

Love, Love, and More Love

I woke up today thinking that love really does cover all. It's so much better to give the benefit of the doubt, to hope for the best, to reserve judgment, to imagine how it is for the other person, to allow the one you love to be who they actually are (not the image you wish they were), to give grace, to have sympathy, to find common ground, to be charitable, to celebrate someone else, to choose delight over dissatisfaction.

There are times to draw boundaries or to put distance between you and someone toxic. Yes. But even then, a little love from behind the self-protecting wall isn't unwarranted—you can at minimum recognize that the person suffering in their brokenness or mental illness or addiction can't possibly be happy with who they are in that state.

In the meantime, slather a little love on yourself, while you're at it. It's a good day to be good to you.

Love, love, love.

Quote of the day

Sustaining thought

All you really need is *love*—or at the very least all you really need is the willingness to love—yourself and others.

Brave Writer

Day 28

No Defense Needed

Try not to defend your life to others. It's tempting to explain your choices, to provide evidence that you did the best you could or that your convictions are pure and your motives are selfless.

We're all a bundle of needs, making decisions that are both selfless and self-interested. The only criteria that matters in evaluating how you spent today is the one you've chosen to live by—today.

That criteria shifts and changes. Some years you have more energy for self-sacrifice and understanding, and others, you find you need someone to give you a break, to make up for what you don't have, to be the strength you lack. Some years you find resources and help, and others, it seems no one "gets" what you're going through and it's entirely up to you to figure out the way forward.

Some years you're blindsided by facts you never imagined would be the substance of your life, of your family.

We have our ideals (they matter) and we have our limits (they matter too). One person (you, me) can change the entire dynamic in a home by making better, more emotionally supportive, empathetic choices; but it's also true that one person can wreck the peace, by not cooperating, asserting a will that is unresponsive to the best care and kindness you can give.

A family is an interdependent system—no one person can carry it alone. There must be give and take, support and nurture for each person, even if in uneven doses at times.

All you can do is become the most healthy version of you that you can be—taking care of your welfare so that you don't wake up one day and "flip out."

You'll be given good advice: Be generous. Give. Share. Listen. Pay attention. Make adjustments. Become a partner to your kids, to your spouse. Forgive. Find the good, the true, the pure. Let go of petty resentments and high expectations.

But you also need to take care of yourself. Be sure that you, the caregiver, receives care too—by someone, somehow, somewhere. It's how you keep going.

When you hit your limits, you'll get advice to give more. You'll be told what the ideals are. You'll be reminded of your original goals. You'll try harder. We women are especially likely to take this advice to heart.

Just remember: in the trying (which is right and noble and good), stand up for yourself too. You matter as much to the whole system, as all the people you love and serve freely every day.

 Brave Writer

Be good to yourself, no matter what that looks like. You get one life, too. It needs to be a good, peace-filled, lovely one. No Joan of Abeccas here. No Teresa of Calculadders allowed.

Stay connected to your well being while you give to the ones you love.

That's it. Good night.

Quote of the day

Needed this tonight! Thank you!

Jackie Pierce Nell

Sustaining thought

Without you the system falls apart. Give to yourself so you can give to others—without resentment.

Day 29

On Being a Mother

Oprah featured moms on her show a while ago. The two experts who wrote the book were bubbly, sharp, blond business-type women who wore chic outfits that had never seen spit up or spaghetti sauce stains. They rallied the audience into a frenzy of confessions about motherhood, which variously decried the hardships of this first order of creation occupation.

> *"I hate the fluids of babies: pee, spit up, spilt milk, snot."*

> *"I cried the day I drove to the car dealership to buy a mini-van."*

> *"There were days I wanted to 'send them back to the hell from whence they came'."*

On and on the tales of woe poured from the mouths of devoted parents. Video clips of small kids on bikes, disastrous laundry rooms, "stuffed to the gills" cars with seats and sippy cups floated by, making one wonder why anyone would sign up for the task of mothering, let alone sustain it for decades. Moms confessed things, too, like the one who said she didn't want to wake the sleeping baby by stopping the car for a potty break, but she needed to pee so badly, she took a Pampers diaper, stuck

 © Julie (Bogart) Sweeney | bravewriter.com Brave Writer

it between her legs and let it "go" as she drove. Yeah, I thought that was way more information than I needed to know about her, too.

There was a surprising lack of joy represented in the discussion of mothering. Mostly being a mom was held up as the hardest job on earth, the most demanding, the most self-sacrificing, the most misunderstood and overlooked work on the planet. A kind of shared martyrdom, underdog status united everyone and Oprah, never having mothered anyone, had to declare that indeed, they were right. Mothering equaled sainthood (which we all know implies burning at the stake and smiling through it!).

With my kids in the room, listening to the pain of childbirth and engorged breasts, the relentlessness of little voices, the demands of the small child's need for food, sleep and comfort, the annihilation of a woman's identity and sense of self, I couldn't take it any more.

After all, far from being the hardest job in the world, mothering has been the happiest, most satisfying, life-giving, joyful, rewarding, fulfilling and (dare I admit it?) easiest job I've ever had. Oh sure, the hours suck, there are anguishes deeper than the ocean, there are seasons (years!) of such utter exhaustion you can't imagine ever being rested again … but all those discomforts are easily and unequivocally overturned by my children, themselves.

I punched pause on the DVR to set the record straight:

"Being your mother has been the single greatest joy and privilege of my life: not a burden, not a perennial unrelenting source of emotional and physical agony, not the 'hardest job in the world', not the knee-capping blow to my 'adult individuality.' Nor has it been the thankless, under-appreciated, most overlooked profession these mothers would have you believe. In fact, my sense of personhood, identity, and self-knowledge have grown more through mothering than any business I've started, any degree I've earned, any relationship I've pursued. I thank you for being the best people to ever happen to me."

Then I spewed in bullet style the privileges and unique joys that came with mothering them (all five of them, each one popping into my life like a fresh daisy, every two years for 10 years).

Cuddling: Being your mom meant I got to cuddle someone non-stop for 12 years while sleeping with at least one of you at a time, nursing you, carrying you, holding you, helping you in and out of car seats, and backpacking you. Those cuddles turned into powerful bear hugs, as you became teens and adults.

Sleeping together: There is nothing more divine than a baby who falls asleep on your chest while you fall asleep and the whole world stops while mother and tiny child become fused as one content, quiet, shared being. No meditation, yoga, prayer circle, private retreat has ever come close to

 Brave Writer

providing me with the depth of peace, pleasure, and abiding hope that sleeping with a baby (you!) has given me.

Playing: Board games and hopscotch, dress-ups, face paint, finger paint, walks in the woods, trips to the zoo, picking up bugs, rolling down hills, blowing bubbles, eating too many cookies, watching Arthur on PBS, rewatching Disney movies, cards, chasing a dog in the backyard, trampoline jumping, creek splashing, snowman building, skiing, middle of the night slumber parties, bike rides, soccer in the backyard, soccer on the official fields, ultimate Frisbee. What adult gets to do any of this on his or her 9-5 job? Talk about luxury!

Conversation: Oh it starts off good – why do bubbles float? How did I get red hair? Why doesn't Santa Claus visit Moroccans, too? But boy does it keep getting better! I've learned about human rights, veganism, Role Playing Games, Shakespeare, Klingon, fashion, exercise, lacrosse, birds, fantasy novels, conspiracy theories, atheism, feminism, linguistics, alternative monetary systems for world peace (serious!) and more by talking to my kids. Mothering is the job that means taking the dog and kids for a walk in the woods is **on task**. It's the one where teatimes and picnics are considered achievements worth trumpeting to friends and family. It's the job where even on bad days, someone tells you "Hey, I love you, Mom" and then hugs you so tightly, you believe it.

There is no comparison to the jobs I've had in business and writing.

Sure, affirmation and personal achievement are nice—but they are nothing like the bond that comes from the devotion of loving people who live every day looking for you to see them for who they are. I've found that the easiest thing in the world is to love my kids. All it takes is entering into their lives on their terms and giving all I've got. I get it all back and more.

Yes, there have been nights where I cried myself to sleep over a non-stop crying toddler or a teenager's emotional pain. There are times when I feel out of control and invisible and fearful for my child's future or welfare. But the rewards of mothering so far outweigh any of its challenges, I can't relate to the repeated refrains of "how hard I have it" simply because I chose to have five kids. Instead, I just feel perennially lucky that my lifestyle has included such richness, tenderness, and connection to immortality through my children.

I think it's time we blew the whistle. Mothering isn't a job. It's a privilege.

Quote of the day

> *I love this!! Perfect timing! Especially after getting about 3 hours of sleep last night because my youngest was up sick and coughing all night! I'm sooooooo tired, but I would never in a million years trade being a mother for anything else in the world!*
>
> *Kristen Yost*

 Brave Writer

Sustaining thought

Your kids are yours. And you're their mom. What a privilege!

Day 30

Pass on Your Expertise

The best education you can give your kids is in the area of your expertise. Sometimes we diminish the value of our skills because we worry so much about the areas where we are weak. We think endlessly about how to teach math, and research all the methods because we lack confidence. Suddenly math becomes the *Most Important School Subject* ever.

We forget to make time to teach our kids to quilt because, heck, we are quilters and it's not that difficult. It must not matter.

But the thing is: if you're a quilter, think of the amazing skill set you'd pass on to both your girls *and* your boys! I remember one of my friends taught her sons to quilt (she had no daughters) and these 12 and 14-year-old boys would get up to work on their quilts even before going off to school each morning (not even homeschooled).

It's really hard to pass on a love of a subject you don't love yourself. It's hard to teach a skill that you don't possess. But it's surprisingly easy to impart what you do know and love! Your family can have its own trajectory, its own flavor based on what you share that is particularly amazing and cool about who you are.

© Julie (Bogart) Sweeney | bravewriter.com   Brave Writer

Obviously in my family, a love of word play is chief among our values. We've cultivated fans of the Bard, kids who can deconstruct poems, who write well and frequently, who use technology with ease, and who are passionate about human rights and foreign languages. We have kids who care about nutrition, and who can steep a pot of tea with the best of them.

We've not successfully imparted plumbing or hanging dry wall or car repair or surfing.

But you might be able to!

I have friends who taught their kids how to completely remodel a home—from wiring, to knocking out walls, to laying tile, to installing carpet. What a gift!

I know a family where cooking is the optimal expression of togetherness. One of those kids went off to college and his chief pleasure is shopping and cooking for his friends.

I know families who hunt, who examine and care for wildlife, who rescue pets, who volunteer in nursing homes, who are political activists, who use math every day in real, practical, engineering ways (and the kids are, as a result, naturals at it). I know families where dissections and experiments are the most enlivening part of home education.

Being good at what you're good at is the right place to start. Keep your talents going. If you are artistic, why wouldn't you devote a big chunk of your homeschooling time to painting, drawing, sculpting, and designing? What a gift you might give your children— one we all will and do envy.

Those hours spent doing that effortless-for-you-stuff *absolutely should take some time in the day that you might be tempted to use for other, harder-for- you-to-impart subjects.*

Absolutely!

Pass on what you know:

- a foreign language
- photography
- building a deck
- training a pet
- baking pies
- sewing clothes
- finishing the basement
- landscaping the yard
- playing tennis
- reading widely
- watching classic films
- appreciating art
- the history of rock n roll
- playing the piano

 Brave Writer

- fashion
- healthy living
- a love of writing
- a love of gaming
- a love for marginalized people
- identifying birds
- travel
- saving money
- starting a business
- organizing groups
- household management
- building a website
- cooking
- knowledge of the law
- hanging holiday lights
- shopping for good deals
- recycling
- surfing, skiing, swimming, running, hiking
- naming the natural world
- arranging flowers
- plumbing
- carpentry
- crafting
- gardening

Any of these and more are worthy of your time! Invest in your kids by passing on your expertise. It's the quickest path to wonderful family bonding, and to that distinct family identity you wish to cultivate.

Families have generational habits of thought and practice that are passed on through your intentional instruction, and your incidental sharing of enthusiasm.

Don't feel guilty about what you lack. Feel inspired! You get to lead your children into the world of your competencies! And that's just plain fun.

Quote of the day

This is so awesome! Being a former sign maker and graphic designer for 17 years, I have taught my kids some of my skills and they love it! Tonight, I was just contemplating about showing them more. Thanks for posting this. I will make it a goal to load Corel Draw into my kids' computers and let them fully explore the program!

Lina Tardif-Simpson

Sustaining thought

Just think! Your kids can carry on your hobbies, passions, and your professions, too—if you share your expertise with them. Then watch them soar—maybe even pass you up.

© Julie (Bogart) Sweeney l bravewriter.com   Brave Writer

Day 31

People First

Are you a Type A mom who finds it difficult to operate without a checklist? Do you find yourself worried about getting it all done?

On the flipside, do you wish you could be more relaxed, but each time you try, the anxiety rises and you don't quite reach that point?

It's difficult to battle who you are—how you naturally interact with the world. Messy people buy the manuals of the naturally organized, thinking they can change if they just have a system. Type A parents want to find a way to relax without feeling like they are lazy.

I say: Work with whatchu got! It's too hard to do a personality-ectomy!

Better to suit your aims to your style.

For instance, if you want to be a more relaxed mom— one who puts the warm fuzzies ahead of the workbooks, change the checklist. See if that helps.

Self-awareness is the first step. Each time you are tempted to push your kids toward what feels like work rather than delight, breathe. Feel your face. Are you smiling? Are your brows furrowing? Get back to connecting with your children. Measure your day (checklist) with a new "Type A" criteria.

Check these off as you do them.

- ☐ Hugged each kid.

- ☐ Made eye contact with one and had a conversation for three minutes.

- ☐ Asked questions of my quiet child to find out more about her process, not her work completed.

- ☐ Played a game.

- ☐ Took a walk.

- ☐ Cultivated silliness (silly voice, body, jokes, puns, dance moves).

- ☐ Put on music.

- ☐ Smiled at my children, each one, at least once.

- ☐ Gave five compliments.

- ☐ Ate tasty foods and noticed the flavors.

- ☐ Let everyone stop working sooner than they expected.

- ☐ Did someone's task for them.

- ☐ Sat next to my child during her hardest subject until she finished it, offering encouragement.

- ☐ Gave myself and kids permission to not do a boring chapter of the workbook.

☐   Left a mess so my children could return to it later to finish the art project or the Lego build or the play fort.

What if you had a checklist like that? Would that help you be a Type A mom who is also more fun?

Try that for a couple of days and see if you find a new groove for your careful personality—one that measures and values connection over work completed. (You are likely to still finish all the work done because that's who you are! But now you'll make room for the other stuff you wish you would do more spontaneously.)

Good luck!

Quote of the day

I used to write "People first" at the top of my To Do list.

Leonie Westenberg

Sustaining thought

When you put people first you're including yourself too!

Day 32

Pick One Thing

It's a new day. What will you do with it?

I suggest picking "one thing." You can't do ten things, and your homeschool won't transform itself over night.

What you want and what creates momentum is a series of deliberate, prepared choices that lead to a sense of accomplishment and satisfaction. You get there one thing at a time.

Pick the subject, practice, habit, or attitude you wish were more present in your home and "do it" or "have it" or "develop it."

Identify the One Thing that is on top of your mind— the one that keeps coming back to you as the one thing you wish you were living or doing.

Then follow the One Thing principles:

1. **Prepare** (ahead of time). Plan a date, purchase, make copies, organize, think about, read literature related to your one thing choice. Gather materials.

2. **Execute** (day of). Follow through with enough time to invest deeply without distraction. Turn off your

© Julie (Bogart) Sweeney | bravewriter.com Brave Writer

phone, shut down your computer, don't answer the door. Be fully present.

3. **Enjoy** (kids and you). Let yourself forget everything else but that experience/lesson. Be here now. Don't do other things simultaneously; don't think ahead to what you will do next. Engage.

4. **Reminisce** (later that day or next week). Talk about what was fun, remember humor, honor connections, recollect what went well. Talk about when you might do it again.

Quote of the day

Aw, but I can't narrow it down! Kidding…what a burden-lifter.

Angela Palomo

Sustaining thought

Oh the joy of picking just one thing—and then seeing it through.

Day 33

Right One for the Job

Bring your most satisfied self to home education. Allow yourself to feel the natural pride that goes with commitment to your kids, the joy that comes from witnessing their firsts, seconds, and thirds, the happiness that is the adventure of shared learning.

Picture yourself waving goodbye to anxiety, to the version of yourself that is not "good enough" and warmly embrace the vision of you that is already the right woman for the job. You are at your best when you believe that you are the right one.

Quote of the day

This brought tears to my eyes. Thank you for this.
And how wonderful would it be if all parents
could feel this way, and share this sense-of-self,
and joy with their children...homeschooler or not?

Jennie Dickerson Gemignani

Sustaining thought

Keep in mind an image of yourself. The caption says: She's the right one for the job.

 Brave Writer

Day 34

Share Your Goals

Today's homeschool thought: Let your kids in on your goals for them.

It's too easy to research, shop, plan, prepare, and then foist those ideas and activities on your kids. They have no context for the reasoning behind the new book or the special activity. Remember: they're schmart! They can understand ideas like, "I thought we'd try this approach because it is 'hands on'" or "I got excited about poetry when I read this blog post. Want to hear it?"

Ask them what they wish they could plan for the year or month or day. Involve their research—what have they heard from friends' families, from their online buddies, from the books they read that sounds fun to try.

Homeschool is not "done" to anyone. It's a journey of shared learning that ought to include all the members in a cooperative search for harmony and growth.

Quote of the day

*Exactly my thoughts, and you put it into words! ...
[S]eriously, you are helping me in my quest to be a
great writer and coach to my kids. Thanks!*

Anna Derksen Friesen

Sustaining thought

Homeschooling feels less daunting when you approach
it as a shared experience of shared goals!

Brave Writer

Day 35

Stay the Course

That big decision you made? Stick with it. It takes time for everyone to settle in, to adapt, to understand the new contours of this unfolding change.

The emotional highs and particularly the lows are part of the movement of this "new thing." The stiff unfamiliarity is temporary—like shoes that need to be worn so the leather straps soften, and the soles mold to your particular feet.

Sometimes there are blisters and sore toes along the way, but eventually, the fit becomes "right."

In the meantime, while everyone gets familiar with the new reality, stay the course.

The tone of your home is set by you. I know how challenging that is. It's all on you—the mood, the energetic field you create—your family looks to you to know if they should worry or trust, if they can be freely happy or ought to be careworn and subdued.

It's exhausting to lead with joy and alacrity; self-doubt is the most natural part of the breaking-in process during the "new thing transition." While you lead, you also monitor (you can't help it!). The undulating emotions are feedback that can at once validate your decision, and then a day later, shoot it in the heart.

Beware: wait 48 hours before making adjustments. Allow the waves of happy and sad to subside before evaluating each aspect of the new thing. Sometimes emotion is vented and over.

Give the new thing a real chance—to become a way of life, not just a "test run." Invest. Believe.

You can tweak—make it your own, do it your way, adapt it to your particular situation. But don't give up too easily. Trust that your hunch was a good one and live into it.

Stay the course—a little while longer, and see what happens.

Quote of the day

Oh, I love this. I need to save it for September. Some big changes planned for next year's homeschool.

Jennifer Breseman

Sustaining thought

It's wise to take on new things slowly and it's also wise not to abandon them quickly. Establish. Test. Try. Decide.

© Julie (Bogart) Sweeney | bravewriter.com   Brave Writer

Day 36

Support Your Geniuses

"Genius often emerges where there is intimate support for it. Shakespeare worked in the intimate supportive community of a strong theater that wanted his next play. Dickinson worked within the intimate community of a family that loved her and protected her time and privacy. Neither of them were seen by their contemporaries as being greatly gifted. It seems truly important that there be a community of support around the artist that protects the making of art" (Pat Schneider *Writing Alone and with Others* xxi).

This quote struck me while working on the Partnership Writing product. What I know about homeschooling families is that they are uniquely intimate. That's not to say there isn't intimacy in families with kids in public or private schools. Rather, home education creates a context where genius can thrive. Why? Because there are no other people on the planet who are as predisposed to recognize the particular genius of children as the parents of those same little people.

Every time I speak, I'm inundated with mothers who share with me the brilliance of their kids—the breadth of imagination, the depth of vocabulary, the surprising accumulation of facts that the parent never saw the child amassing. Over and over again, parents marvel at who lives inside their children's skin.

From that appreciation and perspective—that "what a miracle is my child" posture—writing growth can occur! We are not fighting for success in grammar and punctuation. Our mission is not the proper execution of essays. We are not charged with critiquing and down-dressing our children for what appears to be lethargy or ineptitude.

Our chief mission at home with our children is to discover and articulate their particular brilliances, and then to fiercely protect the space into which they cast their risky thoughts so they may take the tentative steps toward refining that genius, knowing they are emotionally supported and respected.

You get to do that work! Not a school. Not a theater company. But like Emily Dickinson's family, you may provide for your children the emotionally safe, enthusiastically prepared environment that allows for risk-taking, failure, exaggeration, and blossoming—all in one.

Geniuses. That's who you're raising. Make sure you remember that today.

Brave Writer

Quote of the day

Gorgeous, Julie! Thank you! I need to save this and re-read it on tough days.

Amy Vinroot Wilson

Sustaining thought

You have the distinct honor of protecting and encouraging your genuises—your children—into their particular brilliance.

Day 37

Take Personal Inventory

Be the learner you want to see in your children.

Take personal inventory over a cup of coffee or tea. What do you wish you had time to learn/do/be?

Join a Zumba class? Apply to grad school? Read an art history book? Learn to quilt? Read a novel that is for adults? Garden? Read more about a historical moment? Watch *Downton Abbey* Season 1 or A&E *Pride and Prejudice*? Figure out how to calculate the amount of feed you need for the chickens you will hatch next spring?

What can you do related to that aspiration today? Do one thing on your way to that goal: check out the book or movie, go to the website and download the application instructions, visit a quilting store, stop by the library, look up fall plants online, look up math equations.

When can you do it? After lunch during naptime? Tonight after your spouse or partner gets home? You might be tempted to work on your interests when you can get some alone time.

How about right now, in front of your kids, ignoring what they are doing for a few minutes? Just dive in and

 Brave Writer

talk as you go: "I think I'd like to understand the abolition movement better. It's been so interesting reading about the Civil War with you guys. Give me a few minutes. I'm going to put some books on hold at the library." Or "Hey before we get started today, I want to watch one episode of *Sister Wendy's Story of Painting*. I'm curious about art history and know nothing about it. You can watch if you want, or play with Legos. Then we'll start your stuff."

Don't put off your own learning. Your passion for what you want to know is the fuel of your homeschool. It's not just a model (like you don't do it to "demonstrate" passion). You do it because you are interested. You live it because you need it to thrive! Which is what you hope happens to your kids with their interests.

You must make time right in front of your kids to do what interests you. The only reason kids want to be adults is that adults do cool stuff. So do the cool stuff—and don't feel guilty. It's essential to their growth and your well-being.

What will you do/learn/be today?

Quote of the day

I love the sentences: 'The only reason kids want to be adults is because adults do cool stuff. So do the cool stuff.'

Trudy Klassen

Sustaining thought

Learning in front of your children. Now that's cool! It may stimulate them to learn in front of you.

Brave Writer

Day 38

When the Tears Come, the Writing's Done

Who can do anything well while crying?

Can you type while crying? Cook dinner? Make love? Not well.

Tears are an indication that something is wrong. Really wrong. They signal pain: emotional or physical. In writing, emotional pain may be writer's block or fear of making a mistake. Physical pain may be that the hand hurts from squeezing the pencil too tightly, or eyestrain, or physical exhaustion from a poor night's sleep.

Crying is not a sign of laziness or lack of character. Crying is the last release, the final "giving up" and admission of failure.

Crying signals: I need comfort.

When the tears come, the writing's done.

Take a break. Acknowledge your child's feelings. "I see that you're unhappy. Let's talk about this project later."

Offer a hug.

Later, when your child has regained equilibrium, come back to find out what went wrong.

Ask:

- Are you afraid of making a mistake?
- Is it too hard to grip the pencil for ten minutes straight?
- Are you having a hard time spelling?
- Do you wish you could play outside in the sunshine rather than sit at a table?
- Does it feel like you have nothing to say?
- Are you sleepy? Hungry?
- Do you feel pressured by me?

Be an investigator and a comforter. A cup of tea and eye contact will go a long way toward soothing the hurting writer. Remember, writer's block (not a strong will) is the usual reason for writing paralysis.

Writer's block means the child doesn't have access to the words inside. The words are hidden behind anxiety, fear of failure, or a vague sense of the topic (not enough depth in the subject area to be able to write about it meaningfully).

Writer's block is experienced by everyone (prodigies, professors, and pros) and at its most acute, produces tears.

Give oodles of empathy and hugs. Offer a snack (with protein in it). Talk about how to make writing less painful. Take some time to remind yourself of the goal—a free, brave writer who is at ease when writing, not gripped with anxiety and fear.

If you need strategies for unblocking your chronically blocked writers, take a look at *The Writer's Jungle*.

Quote of the day

> *If you get stuck, get away from your desk. Take a walk, take a bath, go to sleep, make a pie, draw, listen to music, meditate, exercise; whatever you do, don't just stick there scowling at the problem.*

> *Hilary Mantel*

Sustaining thought

A cup of tea and eye contact will go a long way toward soothing the hurting writer.

Day 39

The Joy of Shared Reading

I was friends with an 88 year old man named Wayne (father-in-law to my running partner). I visited him at his nursing home until he died in the fall of 2013.

When I first met Wayne, I was reading the novel for The Arrow (*A Long Way from Chicago*). It dawned on me that the story took place in Wayne's hometown: Decatur Illinois. It is set during The Great Depression, the period of Wayne's early childhood.

When I visited him one day, I told him about the book. He asked me to read it to him. We read chapter one and he could not stop laughing. He loved it so much. He also would comment, "Are you sure this is for children?" With good reason! Richard Peck, the author, plays fast and loose with his reader's sense of right and wrong, but always ends right side up.

I haven't read aloud to anyone in years. I enjoyed reading to Wayne so much, I nearly cried at the end of each chapter. To share a book with an engaged audience is a life-giving, rich experience.

Wayne and I exclaimed over the writing, laughed at the jokes, discussed historical details, and compared

 Brave Writer

them to Wayne's memories. We talked about the shifts in values across generations.

Wayne died six months after I began reading to him. I miss him. What an experience.

If your young ones are gone, find someone to read to. It is nourishing for all involved. And I swear, children's novels are the best!

Quote of the day

> *Yes! Reading aloud is valuable to the listener, AND to the reader. My elderly in-laws read aloud to each other all the time, mostly newspapers and magazines, and clearly they are both having a great experience. Thank you, Julie, for the idea that when our time reading aloud to our kids ends, we can find other ways to do so.*
>
> *Julie Kirkwood*

Sustaining thought

Share a story, make a friend. Share a laugh or a tear and create a bond. You're never too young or too old to enjoy a good read with anyone who will listen.

Day 40

Time to Reinvent

Have you ever noticed that you reinvent homeschool every year? You would think, particularly after having one child go through a certain grade level, that when the next child in line hits the same age and stage, you'd have it all dialed. You'd pull out your notes, books, and memories from the first kid and apply them as a template for the next one!

Yet it rarely works that way.

Instead, the next child comes down the pike and you find yourself doubting the old tricks and books.

You've since heard of a sparkly new program that teaches itself and you want to try it.

This child is *so* different from the last one that the old way just wouldn't work.

Sometimes you will be three children in and realize that you never did like that math curriculum and now that you've figured it out, you can't spend *one more day* looking at that hideously designed book with its awful colors and nonsense explanations, no matter how much you spent on it.

© Julie (Bogart) Sweeney | bravewriter.com · Brave Writer

As you grow in your career of home education, you also get smarter. What satisfied you the first year often feels cramped or schoolish to the new brave you that sees learning through new eyes. You feel freer to risk, to try avant garde strategies. You stop quantifying the hours of the day and allow yourself to "count" card games and nature hikes as part of your children's education.

A mother of nine children (two of them grown and raising their own kids) said over the phone that she was unsure what writing program to buy. She'd already successfully reared, homeschooled, and married off two kids yet was not quite sure if she had the best writing plan for the last two still at home.

If anyone should be at ease in this home education business, you'd think it would be a mother who could reassure herself that with two successful homeschool grads, she must be doing a good enough job with the tools she's already got!

But that's not how it works.

The truth is: we homeschooling mothers are on a never-ending campaign to do right by our children.

That means we tirelessly turn over rocks looking for the next best rightest, brightest choice for this specific child at this specific stage of life.

Not only that, we're a part of the equation too. We want to be stimulated.

We look for triggers for our creativity, we feed our learning curve new ideas and philosophies, we expand our sense of fun and imagination, and we want reassurance that we are making measurable progress with our children.

To that end, homeschooling parents reinvent their homeschools every single year.

It's a part of the warp and woof of this lifestyle. It's what enables parents to sustain twenty-year commitments. It's what creates tailor-made educations that accommodate the wide variety of people in our families.

As you spend time researching what you'll do next year, allow yourself to go on the adventure of reinvention.

Ask yourself five questions to stimulate your thinking:

1. **What works? How do I feel about it?**

   (If it works, you don't necessarily have to change it. But if it works and you are sick of it or the child is bored or you're going through the motions, it's fine to change it up—even if it's "working" in theory.)

2. **What's not working? What can I do about it?**

   (If it's not working, you may need more than a new book. You may need a whole new perspective or view of how to work with this particular subject. Read about the philosophy of education with regard to this subject area and shift how you see it.)

 Brave Writer

3. **What do I wish I were doing that I'm not?**

   (Try doing it for a month or more—to see! Take a small bite of the apple. You don't have to take it in all the way—yet.)

4. **What am I doing that I wish I weren't?**

   (Can you give it up for a week, a month, or reduce it to just a couple times a week? See how that feels?)

5. **What do my kids wish we were doing that we aren't?**

   (Get it on the schedule—plan it, do it!)

Enjoy reinvention. No guilt. No self-doubt. It's one of the many great rewards and satisfactions of being a career home educator.

Quote of the day

> *Coming to the end of this first full year of homeschooling, I needed that pep talk. I want to go out on a limb and do some things on my own and am unsure about some things wondering if they're working and what my children need. I think they'll survive though.*
>
> *Amanda Austin Randolph*

Sustaining thought

Take on the adventure of reinvention and see where it takes you and your kids!

Day 41

Once They Catch On, Look Out!

"My kids are getting it!" I'm seeing this theme come through on Facebook, in email, and through phone calls. What are these kids getting? That what is going on inside (the mind life) deserves a home on paper.

As parents hear their children's thoughts expressed in oral language and help those thoughts get to paper, more and more kids take the risk to cut out the parent-step and try it for themselves.

It's crazy, really. We spend all this time explaining how important writing is, we tell them to follow X model or imitate Aesop or just write three lines, and they show us their sad, uncooperative faces instead. The brilliance of their quirky personalities is hidden behind attempts to sound like someone else. Everyone is demoralized.

Yet if we flip the script—start hearing what our kids are saying in that spontaneous not-school moment, jot down what they say out of our own enthusiasm to preserve the insight, thought, joke, or snatch of story—they perk up.

This is what you wanted me to write? is the thought. You think what I have to say is important enough to write on paper? is the next thought.

 Brave Writer

Young children, especially, will respond with, "Well in that case…" behaviors. They will scratch images and misspelled words onto sheets of paper trying to impress you again! You will be impressed. This child who "didn't know what to write" suddenly has things to say—on paper!

The spelling, punctuation, and capitalization of the words will seem so much less important (and rightly so) when you see the child taking such initiative. Your only task is to fan the flame! Enthuse, supply cool writing utensils, create little booklets (paper folded in half, stapled between a sheet of construction paper), and READ the results aloud to the child and anyone else in the family who will listen.

The momentum this process creates is entirely different than required writing at a desk every day.

A couple necessary caveats

1. For reluctant writers who don't trust you (because they feel the weight of pressure coming from you), adopt a bored gaze (this is for parents whose kids get suspicious when they effuse too much). When you hear them expressing, show enthusiasm and jot it down. But when they write on their own, simply acknowledge it matter-of-factly and then ask hours later if you can read it. Ask plainly without over stating how proud you are so there is room for this child to enthuse or even dislike his or her own work. Then, when you do read the writing, praise the content by engaging it—"I love how the

princess gets out of trouble" or "I didn't know that about amphibians."

2. Writing programs that teach kids to copy other writers (imitation) sometimes stunt the writing voice. Initially your young writer may look like he or she is imitating a style more than showing his or her natural writing voice. Time will heal this tendency the more you support and encourage the natural speaking voice to show up on paper by capturing and recording it.

3. Pictures are writing too! Any attempt to symbolize language is writing. So if a child is writing "picture books" without words, affirm the child as writer! As we know, there are loads of wordless books on the market (we find them in libraries). Ask your child to "read" the book back to you. You'll discover so much thought life and language happening in those pictures. As the child gains skill, words will begin to emerge too.

4. Passion for writing comes in bursts. It's a creative activity. A child may write sixteen little books in a month and then nothing for six months. Do not treat writing like an onerous task. Treat it like the creative outlet that it is! You can always gin up more enthusiasm for writing by changing the setting (write somewhere else, use new utensils, add brownies, change the time of day to write).

5. Read what they write during the read aloud time. Put the finished products in the library basket and

 Brave Writer

read them each day. Most kids love this! Those who don't, honor their choice to not be read aloud.

Above all: value what your kids express and get some of it into writing.

Quote of the day

Thank you for sharing! I have found this method to be true with nearly any subject! It is way more fun and inviting.

Heidi Marie Gillihan

Sustaining thought

Discover the writer within your child and his or her true voice by encouraging self-expression on topics of interest and putting those words on paper.

Day 42

I'm Grateful for My Homeschool

I love this long thread of gratitude. I'm thankful for it.

Brownies? Getting ready for our first teatime in a while—we actually used to do it when the kids were littler. I just picked up Brave Writer last week, and realized we never should have stopped! Thanks for re-setting my expectations so I could relax and have fun again. ~ *Katie Kearns*

My husband who supports me and has conversations with me and urges me to continue breathing. ~ *Julie Yen*

Air conditioning (sorry, but it's true!) ~ *Chloe Field*

Books (I am a sucker for great children's literature). ~ *Tammy Wahl*

Freedom! ~ Christa Bauman

Abundance. ~ *Rhonda Tinkham*

The awesome kids! ~ *Erica Johns*

Flexibility. ~ *Carmen Cox Ledford*

Brave Writer

Freedom to speak about God. ~ *Michelle Schwager Hanks*

My husband! (He has the kids at his parents' and did math with them this morning!) ~ *Farrar Miles Williams*

Vacation time. ~ *Debbie Callander*

Endless possibilities. ~ *Courtney Dunlap*

Understanding and applicability. ~ *Melissa Jackson*

Fexibility! ~ *Micah Hayhurst-Morris*

Creativity flowing. ~ *Becky Rhoads Schick*

Peace. ~ *Melissa DeAnne Molstad*

The flexibility. ~ *Tabitha Forrester McDaniel*

The freedom to make the best choices for everyone. ~ *Cheri Wilbur Nixon*

FLEXIBILITY! ~ *Jacqueline Bay*

Laughter. ~ *Michelle D. Gregory*

Space for exploration and surprise. ~ *Stephanie Beck Borden*

The children! ~ *Amanda Volenec Anderson*

Flexibility. ~ *Jodi Buntin*

Freedom! ~ *Laurie Leavitt-Arcadi*

Whiskey! ~ *Korin Mattei*

Sustaining thought

Freedom and flexibility win!

Brave Writer

Day 43

Trust Your Instinct

One of the most frustrating aspects of being a home educator is that you often have the right ideas, but you get sidelined by "the ghost of public school past," the homeschool forum you are on, the complicated agenda of the program you bought, or the googled descriptions of disorders that you are now pasting over your fabulous child.

I have noticed in my daily phone calls with moms that most have excellent instincts about what their kids need. I know they are on the right track when I hear them say, "It just felt right to help her. She seems so much more confident now" or "I noticed that he responded well when I asked his opinion" or "I just decided to chuck that book! It made everyone miserable!" or "I knew grammar instruction was a waste of our time this year!" or "She does so much better when I let her work independently."

You know your child. You know your family. You know what keeps people happy and at peace. Trust yourself. What do you have to lose? Test your idea with your child and see what happens when you do. Then make adjustments. But start from your hunches, your inner knowing.

Quote of the day

Being the only one among our friends and family who homeschool it always feels like public school is lurking around! I know I feel a lot of worry with our move from Canada to the U.S. I feel out of my element and now have to show everyone HERE that we know what we are doing. Thank you for reminding me that I DO know my kids!!

Lisa Reinsch Johnson

Sustaining thought

No one knows your kids better than you. Trust your instinct. It won't lie.

Day 44

Value Your Child's Voice

We talk quite a bit about writing voice in Brave Writer. We want the writing your kids do to sound like them—to have their vocabulary, inflection, quirky personality, and sense of humor. We don't want them to sound like a copy of Aesop or the writer of X, Y, Z curriculum. We don't want them to produce rote writing where no one can tell who wrote it, so devoid of voice it is.

So we start with freewriting.

But what happens when we give freedom to express and little shows up? What if what we find on the page is lifeless and dull, the utter opposite of what we hear in the bathtub or at an amusement park?

Even worse: what if what comes out really does in fact, sound like your child, but it's lifeless and dull (according to you) and feels like the barest beginnings of original thought?

Time to back up a step.

Writing voice is two words. The real word we want to explore is "voice" all by itself.

Peter Elbow (my guru) describes it this way:

"Most children have real voice but then lose it. It is often just plain loud: like screeching or banging a drum. It can be annoying or wearing for others. 'Shhh' is the response we get to the power of real voice.

"But, in addition, much of what we say with real voice is difficult for those around us to deal with: anger, grief, self-pity, even love for the wrong people. When we are hushed up from those expressions, we lose real voice."

Here's where we sometimes go wrong as parents. We are busy, our children are young and inexperienced. When they risk saying what they really think in the ways they want to really say what they think, we sometimes move into what I call "civilize the savages" mode. We are more worried about the appearance of what they say than what it is, in fact, they are saying.

If your children develop the habit of shutting down their real ideas, thoughts, preferences, wishes, and dreams around you, they will also turn off "real voice." Then when you go to writing with them, they will turn to you and expect you to tell them what words ought to fill the page, just like they now wait for you to show them what thoughts are acceptable to say out loud.

Writing is a risk, but so is speaking. We must create space for both the prudent, acceptable, "makes Mama proud" words and the "Oh I hope she doesn't really feel that way" words. We need to pause and let the rumble of language flow through our kids verbally and they must

 Brave Writer

know that you are interested, receptive, and open-minded enough to hear it (without freaking out) in order for them to find their written voice.

You can start today: eye contact and a focused minute of conversation where you really hear what one of your kids is saying is the beginning of fostering an environment where what your child means to say becomes the norm for what is written.

You also may have to change your own perceptions of what writing is. It may be that you use an artificial voice when you write—the one the teacher told you sounded more grown up, or the one that keeps you from being perceived as impolite, or the one you use to project a cheery disposition.

Maybe you don't even write because the risk feels too great and you avoid it.

Take some time to explore how much space there is in yourself, in your children, and in your home to express authentic voice (verbally first, in writing second). See what you can do to expand that space.

Baby steps:

- "You look angry—want to tell me about it? Want to yell about it?"

- "Your giggly, silliness is cracking me up! I want to be as silly as you!"

- "It's okay to be really sad right now. Tell me about it."

- "I hate that too, sometimes."

- "You are so smart using all those big words!"

- "I would love to hear you tell me more about that story! Go for it. I want every tiny detail." (Instead of insisting on summary)

See what happens. I know for me, I have to put my phone down and walk away from the computer. I also find that it's easy to tune out my kids when the topic doesn't interest me or they are struggling to find the words. I have to remind myself to pay attention and to care. You can't do it every time, but you can do it some of the time, for each child in a rotating way. Be mindful and conscious.

Quote of the day

> *Your voice is damped out by all the interruptions, changes, and hesitations between the consciousness and the page. In your natural way of producing words there is a sound, a texture, a rhythm—a voice—which is the main source of power in your writing…this voice is the force that will make a reader listen to you, the energy that drives the meaning you seek to convey to your readers.*
>
> *Peter Elbow*

Sustaining thought

Let your voice be heard—one word at a time.

 Brave Writer

Day 45

When in Doubt, Remember

When you wonder how to handle that crisis with your child, stop. Remember: how would you have liked your parent to react to you, in a similar situation?

It takes a moment to shift from responsible adult to the memory of vulnerable child or curious middler or risk-taking teen. It's a felt sense, more than a logical thought process.

Re-inhabit the child you were. Go small. Imagine your limited awareness, your feeling of anxiety that you were "in trouble" or that your parents were "going to kill you" or your disappointment in yourself that you had failed to live up to your parents' expectations.

What did you want from them? (Ignore for a moment the temptation you have as a parent to teach lessons, or give consequences, or explain mistakes.) Instead, imagine the tone you wished your parent had taken, or the path to redemption your parent may have offered, or the help the parent could contribute to alleviate pressure or danger or lost opportunities.

Carry on an imagined dialog of how your parent might have handled a crisis that would have helped you. Or recall the caring conversation your parent did have with you that helped you.

Once you've helped yourself "re-feel" what it was like to be young and in trouble, make the subtle shift. Imagine how you might be the "parent-you-wished-you-had" for your child now, in her crisis.

We like to say in Brave Writer:

- Offer help, because help helps.

- Be kind—even if you have to issue consequences, you can still do so with gentleness, kindness, sympathy, and awareness of pain.

- If you are looking for remorse or regret in your child and don't see it, remember how most kids use hardness as a posture to ward off a parent's intensity. If you reach out in the opposite spirit, you may catch your child off guard and find that he or she opens up to you or lets down and shows fear or anxiety or self-recrimination.

- When in doubt, remember who you were, what you wanted, how you felt in crisis, and how you hoped your parent would respond to you.

Go and do likewise.

© Julie (Bogart) Sweeney | bravewriter.com　Brave Writer

Quote of the day

What a great wake up call and reminder. Sobering. Thank you for being our conscience today.

Elke Umbach Holly

Sustaining thought

Remember who you were (and are now) and give your child the compassion and understanding you received or so desperately needed.

Day 46

When Your Kids are Unhappy, What Can You Do?

Over the course of your 10-20 year homeschool odyssey, your kids are going to be unhappy at times. Some of the unhappiness will last months (maybe a year!). Sometimes you're unhappy and it bleeds into the family culture. Here are a few suggestions for how to address some of the boredom and crankiness that visits the various ages and stages of children in your house.

Kids express unhappiness the way kids do:

- boredom

- anger

- fidget-i-ness

- being silly

- procrastinating

- pretending not to listen

- picking on a sibling or the family dog

- tears

- staring blankly out a window

- arguing

© Julie (Bogart) Sweeney | bravewriter.com

- campaigning for what they think will make them happy
- calling someone else a bad name
- doing poorly executed work
- not caring
- not investing
- giving up
- pretending to be happy when they really aren't
- showing signs of stress and anxiety (sleeplessness, restlessness, not interested in eating)
- comparing your home to someone else's
- rejecting your values
- siding with the other parent who momentarily seems more fun

A 4-5 year old who is bored is much easier to rescue than a teenager who feels suffocated and has decided to challenge the values of the family. Yet the underlying feeling is similar—it's unhappiness—and we can facilitate a huge turn around in how our kids experience our homes and "schools" if we help them become peaceful, cooperative, empowered-from-within, happy kids again.

Tuning Into Your Child

Any child who is unhappy needs a parent to tune in and take notice! You're the adult: you get to set aside your agenda to find out what your child needs. The **toddler** needs physical touch and expression of energy (hugs, tickles, eye contact, being flipped upside down, wrestling, chasing, jumping up and down on a bed) to get the adrenaline flowing, to feel reconnected, to up-end a mood. Sometimes food, sometimes a nap, sometimes a cuddle on the couch is enough.

The **young child** benefits from focused attention on his or her specific interests. Too much time spent on your agenda will lead to tedium and crankiness. Bend low to make eye contact first. Then: a board game, running around the back yard, sitting in your lap for a picture book, helping you set the table for a snack, playing on the floor, singing to a CD… These help pull the young child out of the helpless, resentful mood of too many days in a row of someone else's agenda.

The **middler** needs a dedicated time regularly (every day? every other day?) where there is no limit (reading as long as he or she likes without having to do anything else or without being required to sleep, playing a computer game without a timer ending the turn, watching TV and lying on the couch without having to get up, being allowed to finish the entire math book because he's on a roll, digging a hole in the backyard as deep and wide as she likes, taking a scandalous amount of time to organize a bookshelf or rearrange the bedroom furniture, going to the zoo or the museum or the park or the nature preserve to indulge whatever interest is currently on fire, practicing a musical instrument for an entire day). *Middlers are*

© Julie (Bogart) Sweeney | bravewriter.com   Brave Writer

curious. They benefit from indulgence in their curiosity and they especially appreciate it when you "get it." If you notice that a particular child is obsessed with a hobby right now, take advantage of that white heat of passion and let them go!

Buy a book, or rent a DVD, or take a field trip, or purchase new equipment, that adds meaning and energy to the passion. (And yes, I include the Wii, XBox 360, online gaming, and Play Station in this list of "passions" just like I include an absurdly long time of pining for American Girl Doll accessories while paging through a catalog. I've seen good stuff come from these sources in kids.)

The **young teen** is often the most moody and the hardest to cajole out of the mood. Hormones are raging and they are old enough to feel the "been there, done that" of homeschool. They're looking for adventure, yet they are not quite old enough to take charge and make it happen. Try a conversation about **BHAGs** (Big Hairy Audacious Goals). Ask them if there were no monetary limits and no time limits and no travel limits, what they'd like to do? You might find out that your teen wants to take piano lessons for the first time, or join a sports team, or a theater troupe, or learn Klingon, or go to Space Camp, or become expert at fashion.

You may not cure the moodiness, but you can facilitate a brand new, grown-up adventure to buffer the sense of tedium that encroaches at ages 13-14. Talk to the teen! Find out what's missing. Do the best you can to help it happen (you might need that teen to earn money or find someone to drive them or to start small and build—but put that goal somewhere visible and all of you work toward it).

The **older teen** is nearly at adulthood and feeling the tug between wanting a "mommy" and wanting to be respected as a "fledgling adult." Risk and adventure. That's what they need. Let them lead you into conversations about their interests, their viewpoints that aren't yours, their anxieties. These conversations happen best one-on-one, with yummy food or drinks. Make time for the older teen and remember: they are gone A LOT! So if one comes home at midnight ready to talk, you get the toothpicks out to prop your eyelids open and you sit on the bed and talk. The older teen sometimes needs to challenge how he or she was raised and you need to go soft inside and let those words slide over you. They aren't the final verdict. They are the words of a "near adult" trying to find his or her way this week. Be interested, be quiet, be curious, be gentle, be willing to take it.

Bottom Line

You can't keep everyone happy all the time and be happy yourself. Not possible! What you can do is pay attention, remind yourself that these years are fleeting (no matter how today feels), and that **the needs of your children are reasonable and real**. Just like yours. You may not fix any of it in a day, but you can do One Thing today to help

© Julie (Bogart) Sweeney | bravewriter.com   Brave Writer

alleviate some of the building pressure in the home. If you have Many Children (like so many homeschoolers), you'll need help! Tag team with the co-parent or a friend. Get the community involved (youth workers, coaches, aunts and uncles, grandparents).

Take Care of You

You need to be happy too: vitamins, exercise, therapy (it helps if you need it!), time alone, a passion or hobby, a good relationship with your significant other, and a source of joy each day (tea, flipping through a magazine, bubble bath, chocolate, gardening, your favorite rerun on TBS, your spiritual practice).

You can do it!

Quote of the day

Thank you for reminding me what my ultimate goal is: to be their advocate/partner and to grow lifelong lovers of learning! Oh, how I wish I could go back and re-do my oldest child's early years. Unfortunately, that is not possible so I will just have to start where we are right now.

Laura

Sustaining thought

Happy feelings come and go—and so do unhappy feelings. Keep your eye on the moment and give a little extra time and attention to the moody child. Soon he or she will come around and your household will feel like home again.

© Julie (Bogart) Sweeney | bravewriter.com

Brave Writer

Day 47

Why I Homeschool

The holiday season is uniquely challenging to homeschoolers. All fall, you've blissfully gone along planning your days, teaching your children, enjoying the closeness of family learning unaware that anyone outside your four walls would suspect you of inflicting harm or undermining your children's social skills or academic prowess.

Enter Thanksgiving or Christmas or other holiday.

The "non-homeschooling" contingent will assemble and take over for the "state" on your behalf. While passing the glazed carrots to little Theo, Aunt Tilda might quiz: "What's two times six, darling?"

Not to be outdone, your mother-in-law will probe sixth grader Emily: "Do you get out much, sweetheart? Have you any friends?"

Your father will subtly remind you that you haven't got a degree in education and with the economy the way it is, wouldn't it be wiser to get a part time job in your specific field to help support your husband rather than wasting your time all day in the house? Finally, your brother (whose wife works full time outside the home) wonders how you can stand to be with your kids all day, every day.

We don't need certification or testing because our families do a wonderful job of it all by themselves! If you come from a family that supports your homeschooling experience, rejoice and make them extra pumpkin pies! They are the wonderful few (I come from such a family and am deeply grateful).

Even if your family is supportive, you may find yourself at a Christmas party where other adults pretend curiosity about your choice to homeschool while conveying thinly veiled skepticism about your qualifications (yes, that happens to me frequently).

I have a few tips for sticking up for this renegade lifestyle you radical parents have chosen on behalf of your kids.

1. Don't justify your choice by touting your credentials or qualifications.

Even if you have a teaching background, leave it out of the equation. The homeschooling movement benefits from a bold declaration that parents are adequate to teach children to read, handwrite, and calculate times tables. Let skeptics know that you are as much educational coordinator as instructor, as your kids get older. Remind them that they are making educational choices on behalf of their children too!

 Brave Writer

2. Focus on the enjoyment you get from being with your kids.

More important than discussing the failures of the school system is emphasizing how much you love being with your kids. No one can take that away from you. Most parents are startled to realize that being with your own children 24/7 is a pleasure, not a dreaded task. To argue with you means they are admitting they don't enjoy being with theirs in the same way.

3. Talk about 'family learning' instead of school or education.

Many parents imagine assignments, grades, and lectures when they think of homeschool. They can't picture imposing all that discipline and structure, while retaining a happy family atmosphere.

Homeschool is different than institutional learning because the family is learning together. Discuss how everyone gets involved at his or her own level when working on a history topic or science experiment, when freewriting or listening to a novel read aloud. Tell them about tea times and poetry. Resist the temptation to explain how what you do matches what a school requires.

4. Validate their authority in selecting the educational choices they've made for their kids.

This is perhaps the most important thing you can do—talk about educational choice. All of us make choices in how we educate our children. Let them know that you support their enthusiasm for the school system and that you can see how that's working out for their kids (find whatever good is occurring in their lives and support it). Then share the unique joys of homeschool.

5. Resist defending your kids' social lives.

That one rarely goes anywhere good. We've all been programmed since toddlerhood to believe that socialization matters and that it happens at school. Trying to get adults to understand differently is an exercise in clacking your noggin against a cutting board! So side step it like this: "My kids have great social lives. You know us. We're into people, just like you!" Something to the effect that lets them know that you aren't worried one tiny bit about their futures as successful people in the world.

6. Don't bash school.

Surefire way to set off fireworks over the mashed potatoes. Focus on what you love about homeschool, share one or two challenges (if appropriate) so that you don't sound like a propaganda machine, and affirm your relatives for the great kids they have.

We are all insecure about our choices so be a voice that lets your family know that you support them in their parenting, too! (If you aren't impressed with their parenting, the holidays are not the time to bring that up!)

© Julie (Bogart) Sweeney | bravewriter.com Brave Writer

7. Take responsibility for the outcome of homeschool.

I always like to remind inquiring people that I know I took a risk by keeping my kids home. I tell them that I didn't know how it would all turn out, but I was willing to take a chance and make corrections as I went. I even say that my kids may make different decisions for their own children when they are older. I avoid committing to superior learning, better college admittance scores, and brilliance in my offspring, or anything that puts pressure on my kids to be poster-children for homeschooling. They don't need it or deserve the scrutiny. I take all the skepticism on to me, and I let the failure they may associate with my homeschool choice fall on my head. Protect your kids. Don't tout their astounding brains because Aunt Shirley will immediately conjure a pop quiz.

8. Don't talk to rude people.

Turn away insulting comments with a polite, "I'd rather not talk about homeschool on my Thanksgiving vacation. This is my time off. Curmudgeons don't deserve the full "why I homeschool" defense.

The bottom line is this: You homeschool because it feels like the best educational choice for your family. That's a good enough reason for everyone. And you can stop right there, if you need to. There's always the remote control, pie, and football to distract the persistent.

Quote of the day

Great list! I particularly like #7. One way I've responded to questions is to simply say that each form of education has strengths and weaknesses. I'll give what I see as the strengths and weaknesses of learning at home as we've done it. Many times questions aren't hostile; people are only trying to understand. (I've answered LOTS of questions from friends who are Chinese and are fascinated by the very foreign concept of homeschooling!) I also think your point about family learning is a great one! It's very difficult for some people to get away from education as bells and tests and large classrooms filled with children who listen.

Becky Parker

Sustaining thought

Homeschooling is a choice just as much as public or private school is—no defense needed.

Day 48

Why Study Literature?

The study of literature is intended to give students a lens into the ideas and stories that shape society (present and past) as well as to expose them to the complexity of human development, through time. All sorts of fiction genres create scaffolding for philosophies, ideologies, the politics of relationships, the exploration of the logical end of imagined scenarios, the psychology behind particular actions and events, and more. Literature also exposes students to uses of language not available in non-fiction, and creates a series of cultural touchstones for shared understanding that transcend mere fact.

In short, literature provides an avenue of expanded imagination and language for the sake of both appreciating beauty and human depths, while sharing the experience with other readers (creating a kind of connection and community through shared story). We consider the reading of literature to be one of the ways we create societal cohesion!

Now onto the real question: do they have to study it?

Kids don't have to study lit any more than they have to study trigonometry or post-modernism or physics or sculpture. Some exposure to literature is valuable just like some exposure to advanced math and science has value. But for kids who are not enamored with literature, keep it to a minimum just like you would if you were raising an actress who never imagined using the quadratic equation in her future but who wanted to go to college and so needed to take Algebra 2.

Make it as painless as possible. Select works of fiction that are more easily accessible (popular story lines with fast-paced writing). Learn how to identify themes, imagery, plot arc, and characterization. Appreciate the use of language (note what sort it is, examine why it works or doesn't).

Learn to write one literary analysis essay in high school so when it happens in Freshman English in college, it won't be your child's first attempt.

Quote of the day

Julie, I always love your approach to teaching. You assess what is important and then tailor the level to the need of the student. I try to do that as well, but I am not nearly as eloquent as you are. Often, I haven't even articulated the ideas to myself, much less my children. You put words to things in a way that allows me to think more deeply about those ideas. Thank you for sharing your gifts with us.

Ann Herndon Corcoran

Sustaining thought

Literature provides an avenue of expanded imagination and language, which can be shared with others.

Day 49

Why Write Better?

Top reasons to write better:

1. To eliminate the stress associated with writing!

2. To express and externalize feelings.

3. To argue a viewpoint with power.

4. To keep in touch with people you love.

5. To entertain and inform people.

Education (academic writing) is a great process of growth, but its duration of use is short-lived! Remember: cultivating a writer is about ensuring that your adult will be able to function literately in all of his or her activities and relationships!

Quote of the day

These are great motivations and goals to write better. Thanks for the list.

Brenda Story

Sustaining thought

Writing is a skill your kids will use for a lifetime so it's worth learning to write better.

Day 50

Your Child Needs You

Your child needs you, not a scope and sequence. Not tests. Not assignments.

You brought your child home to opt out of a system of cups and pounds, inches and altitudes, teaspoons and litres.

Your child grows—whether you help or not, whether you interfere or guide, support or neglect.

Measuring growth doesn't cause growth. Sometimes, all it does is cause unhelpful worry.

Growing is the job of children—to get tall, to acquire language, to peer into an intriguing world, to sprout beards or body curves.

Your kids will read better, calculate more easily, handwrite with less effort, produce quality insights more frequently, and show curiosity about the fascinating ideas and activities they discover along the way to becoming twenty, because that's what human beings do.

This all happens—while they sleep, and when they wake, and while they bump along, doing what they're told, doing what they do when no one's watching, doing what they love, and resenting what they hate.

 Brave Writer

Sometimes they grow a quarter inch in an entire year (that was me, in sixth grade).

Sometimes they grow six inches in twelve months (that was me, in eleventh grade).

Sometimes they can't read, can't read, can't read—and then they read. At age seven or ten or four.

Sometimes they tell you they hate grammar—and then major in linguistics in college.

You can't stop the growth, even with lightning or flash freezing or wishing they would stay young, adorable, innocent, and easy—a little longer.

You can't make it happen faster by forcing a program that is more advanced or requiring more or worrying and handwringing.

Your kids need you, though. They need you to be amazed by their leaps and bounds, their first steps and first essays.

They need space to "get it" and new ideas to help when they don't.

They need your confidence that they are doing just fine, that they will get there, wherever "there" is.

They need your investment: of money for lessons, of patience for their challenges, of heart when they must be brave.

They need your faith that the work you do together is enough, that you can't stop them from being the fabulous people they are destined to be, even if you tried. They will grow, grow, grow and all you can do is jump in the passenger seat, open the sunroof, and turn up the radio on the joy ride.

Homeschool allows everyone to grow at the only pace they can: theirs.

Homeschool allows you to be present to who they are today, rather than worrying about who school says they should have been by now.

What a privilege.

Quote of the day

> *Thanks, I needed that!! I am in the fourth month of homeschooling my nine-year-old. Pulling him out of public school in Manhattan was a no-brainer, as it just continued on its relentless course of teaching to a test. He is singing and humming now, and that hasn't happened in years.*
>
> *David Ricceri*

Sustaining thought

You are essential to your homeschool more than any curricula. Becoming the best you possible is your greatest gift to your children.

 Brave Writer

# New To Brave Writer?

The principles you've enjoyed in this volume are the ones I use to help you teach writing!

The best tool to transform your writing life is *The Writer's Jungle*. *The Writer's Jungle* is the centerpiece to the Brave Writer lifestyle. In it, homeschooling parents find the insight, support and tools that help them become the most effective writing coaches their children will ever have.

The missing ingredient in writing curricula isn't how to structure a paragraph (information that can be readily found on the Internet). You don't need more facts about topic sentences or how to use libraries. Grammar and spelling are not the key components in writing, either, much to the chagrin of some English teachers.

- Are you tired of the blank page blank stare syndrome (hand a child a blank page; get back a blank stare)?

- Are you worried that you aren't a good enough writer to teach writing?

- Is your child bright, curious, and verbal but seems to lose her words when she is asked to write?

- Do you wonder how to expand the ideas in the sentences your child writes without damaging your relationship?

© Julie (Bogart) Sweeney | bravewriter.com Brave Writer

- Has writing become a place where tears flow and fears surface?

- Is your child a prolific writer and you aren't sure how to direct him to the next level?

- Have you tried "just about everything" and feel ready to give up on writing?

If you answered 'yes' to any of these questions, then *The Writer's Jungle* is for you! Purchase it today.

If you aren't quite ready to make the big investment, get your feet wet with an issue of The Arrow (3rd – 6th grades) or The Boomerang (7th – 10th grades)—intended to help you teach the mechanics of writing naturally and painlessly!

Enjoy your journey to Brave Writing!

Made in the USA
Middletown, DE
05 April 2018